HOW TO STUDY

SEVENTH EDITION

Ron Fry

Course Technology PTR
A part of Cengage Learning

COURSE TECHNOLOGY
CENGAGE Learning·

Australia, Brazil, Japan, Korea, Mexico, Singapore, Spain, United Kingdom, United States

COURSE TECHNOLOGY
CENGAGE Learning™

How to Study, Seventh Edition
Ron Fry

Publisher and General Manager, Course Technology PTR:
Stacy L. Hiquet

Associate Director of Marketing:
Sarah Panella

Manager of Editorial Services:
Heather Talbot

Marketing Manager:
Mark Hughes

Senior Acquisitions Editor:
Mitzi Koontz

Interior Layout Tech:
Judy Littlefield

Cover Designer:
Luke Fletcher

Indexer:
Valerie Haynes Perry

Proofreader:
Sandi Wilson

For product information and technology assistance, contact us at **Cengage Learning Customer & Sales Support, 1-800-354-9706**

For permission to use material from this text or product, submit all requests online at **cengage.com/permissions** Further permissions questions can be e-mailed to **permissionrequest@cengage.com**.

All trademarks are the property of their respective owners.

All images © Cengage Learning unless otherwise noted.

Library of Congress Control Number: 2011923932

ISBN-13: 978-1-4354-5968-7

ISBN-10: 1-4354-5968-7

Course Technology, a part of Cengage Learning
20 Channel Center Street
Boston, MA 02210
USA

Cengage Learning is a leading provider of customized learning solutions with office locations around the globe, including Singapore, the United Kingdom, Australia, Mexico, Brazil, and Japan. Locate your local office at: **international.cengage.com/region**.

Cengage Learning products are represented in Canada by Nelson Education, Ltd.

For your lifelong learning solutions, visit **courseptr.com**.

Visit our corporate Web site at **cengage.com**.

Printed by RR Donnelley.
Crawfordsville, IN. 1st Ptg. 04/2011

Printed in United States of America
1 2 3 4 5 6 7 13 12 11

Contents

Introduction xi

Chapter 1: How to Start Out Right 1

Chapter 2: How to Organize Your Studying 15

Chapter 3: How to Read and Remember 45

Chapter 4: How to Organize Your TIme 75

Chapter 5: How to Excel in Class 101

Chapter 6: How to Conduct Your Research 123

Chapter 7: How to Write Terrific Papers 133

Chapter 8: How to Study for Tests .171

Epilogue 217

Index 219

INTRODUCTION

HOW TO USE THIS BOOK

> "What one knows is, in youth, of little moment;
> they know enough who know how to learn."
> —Henry Adams

L earning how to study is learning how to learn. And that is, to me, the greatest gift you can ever give yourself…or your children.

Having stated that so boldly, I suspect I still have to convince some of you that spending any time trying to master this stuff—studying, learning, reading, note taking, writing—is worth your while.

There are, of course, some terrific reasons why you *should* learn how to study, why you really *must* learn how to study. But before I start convincing you that developing proper study skills *is* important—and why—let's figure out exactly what we mean by "study skills" so we're all on the same wavelength.

Yes, *How to Study* includes hints, advice, and techniques for taking notes in class, while you're reading your textbooks, in the library, and online; how to prepare for tests; and how to organize your study schedule to get the best results in the shortest amount of time. But that's only *half* of the book. There are essential skills you may think have nothing to do with studying, and important steps you need to take right from the start.

Here's Where to Start

> "Learn as though you would never be able to master it;
> hold it as if you would be in fear of losing it."
> —Confucius

Developing great study habits is like a foot race between you and your friends. Before you can declare a winner, you have to agree on where the finish line is. In other words, how do you measure your ability to use these skills? What's good? What's poor?

But you can't even start the race until you know where the *starting* line is—especially if it's drawn at a different spot for each of you!

Chapter 1 starts by explaining individual study skills and clarifying how each can and should function in your life. Then you'll be given the chance to find your own starting line.

In Chapter 2, you'll learn the importance of where, how, and when you study, and you'll start building the study environment that's perfect for *you*. Why is this important? If you've spent three hours reading *Gravity's Rainbow* with Outkast shaking the walls, it's not surprising you're still on page three. Reading about and understanding Mr. Pynchon might have little to do with increasing reading comprehension, rescheduling your time, or changing books...and a lot more to do with just turning down the volume.

There is no magic elixir in the study habit regimen. If math and science are not your strong suits, memorizing *How to Study* will not transform you into a Nobel Prize-winning physicist. Nobody is great at *everything*, but everybody is great at *something*. So you'll also get a chance to rate the subjects you like and dislike, plus those classes you do best and worst in.

Chapter 2 also introduces some of the "intangibles" in the study equation: your home environment, attitude, motivation, and so forth. If you are dedicated to studying and motivated to achieve certain goals, all the other factors that affect your study habits will fall more naturally into place. A belief in the study ethic is one of the keys to success.

Finally, mastering some other key components of the study process—learning to "read" teachers, developing mentors, dealing with perfectionism, the importance of flexibility—will help you get off to the right start.

Reading and Comprehension

Chapter 3 introduces the skills basic to any study process: reading and comprehension. No matter how well you learn to take notes, how familiar you become with your library, how deftly you surf the Internet, how doggedly you study for tests, if you are reading poorly (or not enough) and not understanding what you read, life will be difficult.

Becoming a good reader is a skill, one usually acquired early in life. If it's a skill you haven't acquired yet, now is the time! Chapter 3 also points out how your ability to recall ideas, facts, and figures can be significantly increased (quantitatively and qualitatively) with practice.

Making Up for Lost Time

To see a significant change in your life, most of you will not need to study *harder*, just *smarter*. This means making better use of your study time—spending the same two, three, or four hours, but accomplishing twice, thrice, or four times what you do now. Chapter 4 introduces the simplest and easiest-to-use organizational and time-management tools you'll ever find—powerful ways to make sure you are always on track, including guidelines to develop both short-term and long-term calendars.

Go to the Head of the Class

In Chapter 5 I talk about the one experience we all have in common, no matter how old we are: the classroom. I'll help you take better notes, encourage your active participation in class discussions—including pointers on how to overcome the tendency to hide behind the plant in the back of the room—and help you get a lot more out of lectures.

Becoming an Information Hound

Chapter 6 introduces you to the two important resources in your study career—your library and the Internet—and discusses how to build up your research muscles to get the information you need when you need it. You'll learn about the books, periodicals, newspapers, magazines, computer software, videos, audiotapes, and other reference materials available to you at most brick-and-mortar libraries and suggestions for how to find and use them, including an explanation of the Dewey decimal classification and Library of Congress systems. I'll also cover the use of online resources and the importance of becoming computer and Internet literate.

So You're Not the Next Hemingway

I'm convinced that too many of you place the emphasis in "writing papers" on the word "writing." In Chapter 7 I'll introduce you to a remarkably easy way to take notes and organize your information. By breaking down any paper, no matter how complex, into easy-to-follow steps, I'll help you create papers infinitely better than before—even if you're still no threat to Hemingway (or anybody else) when it comes to writing.

How to "Ace" Any Test

Chapter 8 covers the dos and don'ts of test preparation, including the differences between studying for weekly quizzes, midterms, and final examinations; why last-minute cramming doesn't work (but how to do it if you have no other choice—shame!); studying for and taking different types of tests (multiple-choice, true/false, essay, open book, and so on); how to increase your guessing scores; even which questions to answer first and which to leave for last.

How Smart Do You Study?

How to Study is the most comprehensive study guide ever written— a fundamental, step-by-step approach that *you* can follow to develop and sharpen your study skills.

If you're struggling through college or graduate school, here's your life preserver.

If you're a high school student planning to attend college, *now's* your chance to hone your study skills.

If you're heading for trade school or not even considering college— even if you're ready to drop out of high school at the earliest possible instant, you still need *How to Study*.

If you're an adult returning to the classroom after a lengthy absence, there's no substitute for the tips and techniques you will learn in this helpful collection.

So what if you're a really poor student? How smart you are is not the point. *What counts is how smart you study*.

With the possible exception of the 2 percent of you who qualify as "gifted," the effective study habits *How to Study* teaches will help students of any age and ability level.

If your grades are average to good, you will see a definite improvement. If you are on the borderline of the pass/fail range, you will benefit considerably. If good study habits are in place but rusty as a result of years away from the classroom, *How to Study* will be the perfect refresher for you.

And if you are one of those "gifted" 2 percent, I *still* think you'll find many helpful techniques in these pages.

Who Is This Book Really For?

While I originally wrote *How to Study* for high school students, I've discovered over the years that I could probably count on only a couple of hands the number of such students who actually bought a copy of the book.

The surprise was that so many of the people buying *How to Study* (and writing me reams of letters along the way) were adults. Yes, a number of them were returning to school and saw *How to Study* as a great refresher. And some were long out of school but had figured out that if they can learn *now* the study skills their teachers never taught them (or they never took the time to learn), they will do better in their careers.

All too many were parents who had the same lament: "How do I get Johnny to read (study, do better on tests, remember more, get better grades)? If all his classes were on PlayStation, he'd be an A student!"

So I want to briefly take the time to address every one of the audiences for this book and discuss some of the factors particular to each of you.

If You're a High School Student

You should be particularly comfortable with the format of the book—its relatively short sentences and paragraphs, occasionally humorous (hopefully) headings and subheadings, and the language used. I wrote it with you in mind!

But you should also be *un*comfortable with the fact that you're already in the middle of your school years— the period that will drastically affect, one way or the other, all the *rest* of your career—*and you still don't know how to study!* Don't lose another minute. Make learning how to study and mastering *all* of the study skills in this book your *absolute priority*.

If You're a Middle School Student

Congratulations! You're learning how to study at *precisely* the right time. Sixth, seventh, and eighth grades—before that sometimes-cosmic leap to high school—is without a doubt the period in which all these study skills should be mastered, since doing so will make high school not just easier, but a far more positive and successful experience.

If You're a "Traditional" College Student

...age 18 to 25, I hope you are tackling one or two of the study skills you failed to master in high school (in which case I highly recommend you also read the other books in my *How to Study Program*). Otherwise, I can't see how you're ever going to succeed in college. (Then again, I can't figure out how you managed to get *into* college.) If you are starting from scratch, my advice is the same as to the high school students reading this book: Drop everything and make it your number one priority. Do not pass Go. Do not order pizza.

If You're the Parent of a Student of Any Age

Your child's school is probably doing little, if anything, to teach him or her how to study. Which means he or she is not learning how to *learn*. And that means he or she is not learning how to *succeed*.

There are probably even more dedicated parents out there than dedicated students, since the first phone call at any of my radio or TV appearances comes from a sincere and worried parent asking, "What can I do to help my kid do better in school?" Okay, here they are, the rules for parents of students of any age:

1. **Set up a homework area.** Free of distraction, well lit, with all necessary supplies handy.

2. **Set up a homework routine.** When and where it gets done. Studies have clearly shown that students who establish a regular routine are better organized and, as a result, more successful.

3. **Set homework priorities.** Actually, just make the point that homework *is* the priority—before a date, before TV, before going out to play, whatever.

4. **Make reading a habit**—for them, certainly, but also for yourselves. Kids will inevitably do what you *do*, not what you *say* (even if you say *not* to do what you *do*).

5. **Turn off the TV.** Or at the very least, severely limit when and how much TV-watching is appropriate. This may be the toughest suggestion to enforce. I know. I'm the parent of a teenager.

6. **Talk to the teachers.** Find out what your kids are supposed to be learning. If you don't know the books they're supposed to be reading, what's expected of them in class, and how much homework they should be scheduling, you can't really give them the help they need.

7. **Encourage and motivate,** but don't nag them to do their homework. It doesn't work. The more you insist, the quicker they will tune you out.

8. **Supervise their work,** but don't fall into the trap of *doing* their homework. Checking (i.e., proofreading) a paper, for example, is a positive way to help your child in school. But if you simply put in corrections without your child learning from her mistakes, you're not helping her at all…except in the belief that she is not responsible for her own work.

9. **Praise them when they succeed,** but don't overpraise them for mediocre work. Kids know when you're being insincere and, again, will quickly tune you out.

10. **Convince them of reality.** (This is for older students.) Okay, I'll admit it's almost as much of a stretch as turning off the TV, but learning and believing that the real world will not care about their grades, but will measure them by what they know and what they can do, is a lesson that will save many tears (probably yours). It's probably never too early to (carefully) let your boy or girl genius get the message that life is not fair.

11. **If you can afford it, get your kid(s) a computer** and all the software they can handle. There really is no avoiding it: Your kids, whatever their ages, absolutely must be computer-savvy in order to survive in and after school.

12. **Turn off the TV already!**

13. **Get wired.** The Internet is the greatest invention of our age and an unbelievable tool for students of any age. It is impossible for a college student to succeed without the ability to surf online, and nearly impossible for younger students. They've got to be connected.

14. **But turn off IM (Instant Messaging) while doing homework.** They will attempt to convince you that they can write a term paper, do their geometry homework, and IM their friends at the same time. Parents who believe this have also been persuaded that the best study area is in front of the TV.

The Importance of Your Involvement

Don't for a minute underestimate the importance of *your* commitment to your child's success. Your involvement in your child's education is absolutely essential. The results of every study done in the last two decades clearly confirm the single factor that overwhelmingly affects a student's success in school: your involvement—not money, great teachers, a bigger gym, or weekly dance classes. *You*.

So please, take the time to read this book (and all of the others in the series). Learn what your kids *should* be learning (and which of the other subject-specific books in the series your child needs the most).

And you can help tremendously, even if you were not a great student yourself, *even if you never learned great study skills*. You can learn now with your child—not only will it help him or her in school, it will help *you* on the job, whatever your field.

If You're a Nontraditional Student

If you're going back to high school, college, or graduate school at age 25, 45, 65, or 85—you probably need the help in *How to Study* more than anyone! Why? Because the longer you've been out of school, the more likely you don't remember what you've forgotten. And you've forgotten what you're supposed to remember! As much as I emphasize that it's rarely too early to learn good study habits, I must also emphasize that it's never too *late*.

What You Won't Find in This Book

I've seen so-called study books spend chapters on proper nutrition, how to dress, how to exercise, and a number of other topics that are *not* covered *at all* in *How to Study*, except for this briefest of acknowledgments: It is an absolute given that diet, sleep, exercise, and the use of drugs (including alcohol, nicotine, and caffeine) will affect your studying, perhaps significantly.

Having said that, I see little reason to waste your time detailing what should be obvious: Anything—including studying—is more difficult if you're tired, hungry, unhealthy, drunk, stoned, and so on. So please use common sense. Eat as healthily as you can, get whatever sleep your body requires, stay reasonably fit, and avoid alcohol and other drugs. If your lack of success is in any way due to one of these other factors and you're unable to deal with it alone, find a good book or a professional to help you.

Are You Ready to Learn Something?

The book you are holding in your hands is now in its seventh edition, and has been helping students and parents (and even teachers) for more than 20 years. (The other books in my *How to Study Program—"Ace" Any Test, Get Organized, Improve Your Memory, Improve Your Reading,* and *Improve Your Writing*—are also available in new editions.)

Thank you for making these books so successful.

Learning shouldn't be painful or boring, though it is occasionally both. I don't promise that *How to Study* will make *everything* easier. It won't. It can't. And it may actually require some work to achieve what you want. But *How to Study* will show you the path, give you directions, and make sure you're properly provisioned for your journey.

You will not understand everything the first time you read it. Or, perhaps, even the second or third time. You may have to learn it slowly, very slowly. But that doesn't mean there's something wrong with you. It may be a subject that everyone learns slowly. (My particular nemesis was organic chemistry.) A poorly written textbook or unmotivated teacher can make any subject a torture.

Parents often ask me, "How can I motivate my teenager?" Well, there *is* an answer, but it's not something *parents* can do—it's something you, the student, have to decide: Are you going to spend the school day interested and alert or bored and resentful?

It's really that simple. Since you have to go to school anyway, why not decide that you might as well be active and learn as much as possible instead of wallowing in misery? The difference between a C and an A or B for many students is, I firmly believe, merely a matter of *wanting* to do better. When you graduate, you'll quickly discover that all anyone cares about is what you know and what you can do. Grades won't count anymore; neither will tests. So you can learn it all now or regret it later.

You will also inevitably decide that one or more courses couldn't possibly be of any use later in life. "I don't have a clue why I'm busting my hump to learn calculus (algebra, physics, chemistry, European history, fill in the blank)!" you lament. "I will *never* need it."

Trust me: You have no idea what you may or may not need, use, or remember next *week*, let alone in a decade. I have found in my own life that a surprising amount of "useless" information and learning has been vitally important to my career.

So learn it all. Get excited about the *process* of learning, and I guarantee you will not ever worry about what you need to know in the future.

There Are Other Study Guides

Though I immodestly maintain that my *How to Study Program* is the most helpful to the most people, there are certainly plenty of other purported study books out there. Unfortunately, I don't think most of them deliver on their promises. Inevitably, these other books promote the authors' "system," which usually means what *they* did to get through school. This "system," whether basic and traditional or wildly quirky, may or may not work for you. So what do you do if "their" way of taking notes makes no sense to you? Or you master their highfalutin' "Super Student Study Symbols" and still get Cs?

There are very few "rights" and "wrongs" out there in the study world. There's certainly no single "right" way to attack a multiple-choice test or take notes or write a paper. So don't get fooled into thinking there *is*, especially if what you're doing seems to be working for you. Don't change what "ain't broke" just because some self-proclaimed study guru claims what you're doing is all wet. Maybe he's all wet.

Needless to say, don't read *my* books looking for some single, inestimable system of "rules" that works for everyone. You won't find it, 'cause there's no such bird. You *will* find a plethora of techniques, tips, tricks, gimmicks, and what-have-you, some or all of which may work for you, some of which won't. Pick and choose, change and adapt, figure out what works for you. Because *you* are responsible for creating *your* study system, *not me*.

That said, I *can* guarantee that the nearly 1,000 pages of my *How to Study Program* contain the most wide-ranging, comprehensive, and complete system of studying ever published. I have attempted to create a system that is usable, useful, practical, and learnable. One that *you* can use—whatever your age, whatever your level of achievement, whatever your IQ—to start doing better in school, in work, and in life *immediately*.

I think we've spent enough time talking about what you're *going* to learn. Let's get on with the learning.

Ron Fry

CHAPTER 1

HOW TO START OUT RIGHT

"It is not enough to understand what we ought to be,
unless we understand what we are; and we do not understand
what we are, unless we know what we ought to be."
—T.S. Eliot

Taking a good, honest look at yourself is not the easiest thing in the world. In the next two chapters, I'm going to help you:

- Evaluate the current level of all your study skills, a necessary step to identify those areas in which you need to concentrate your efforts.
- Identify the study environment and learning style that suit you.
- Categorize all of your school subjects according to how well you *like* them and how well you *do* in them.

How to Keep Score

In the next few pages, I'll explain the 11 primary study skills covered in this book: reading and comprehension, memory development, time management, library skills, computer skills, textbook note taking, classroom note taking, library note taking, classroom participation, writing papers, and test preparation. Then I'll ask you to rate yourself on your current level of achievement and understanding of each: "A" (excellent) for mastery or near mastery of a particular skill; "B" (good) for some mastery; "C" (fair to poor) for little or no mastery.

But let's do a "down-and-dirty" test first, just to give you a taste of what's to come. Read the following 28 statements and consider which apply to you. If a statement does apply, mark "Y" (for yes). If not, mark "N" (for no):

1. ❏ Y   ❏ N   I wish I could read faster.

2. ❏ Y   ❏ N   I go to class, but I don't pay a lot of attention.

3. ❏ Y   ❏ N   I rarely review for tests, but I do spend hours cramming the night before.

4. ❏ Y   ❏ N   I think I spend more time studying than I need to.

5. ❏ Y   ❏ N   I usually study with the radio and/or TV on.

6. ❏ Y   ❏ N   I rarely finish all my homework on time.

7. ❏ Y   ❏ N   I usually write assigned papers the week (or the night) before they're due.

8. ❏ Y   ❏ N   I read every book at the same speed and in the same way.

9. ❏ Y   ❏ N   I'm an IM whiz but I can never seem to find the information I need on the Internet.

10. ❏ Y   ❏ N   I'm overwhelmed with too much homework.

11. ❏ Y   ❏ N   I can never complete my reading assignments on time.

12. ❏ Y   ❏ N   I always seem to write down the wrong stuff in class.

13. ❏ Y ❏ N I frequently forget important assignments and test dates.

14. ❏ Y ❏ N I get nervous before exams and do worse than I think I should.

15. ❏ Y ❏ N I frequently must reread whole passages two or three times before I understand them.

16. ❏ Y ❏ N When I finish reading a chapter, I usually don't remember much of it.

17. ❏ Y ❏ N I try to take down everything the teacher says, but usually can't understand any of my notes.

18. ❏ Y ❏ N I can only study for about 15 minutes before I get bored or distracted.

19. ❏ Y ❏ N When I'm working on a paper or report, I spend most of the time with a thesaurus in my lap.

20. ❏ Y ❏ N I always seem to study the wrong stuff.

21. ❏ Y ❏ N I don't use any kind of calendar.

22. ❏ Y ❏ N I study for some tests, but I always forget what I studied when I get there.

23. ❏ Y ❏ N I don't have enough time to do well in school and still have a social life.

24. ❏ Y ❏ N I can't figure out the important points in my textbooks.

25. ❏ Y ❏ N When I look at my class notes right before a test, I can't understand them.

26. ❏ Y ❏ N I hate to read.

27. ❏ Y ❏ N I get marked down on essay tests because I don't organize them well.

28. ❏ Y ❏ N I spend a lot of time on my computer, but it feels like most of it is wasted.

What do your answers mean? If you answered yes to questions:

- 2, 5, or 18, you need to work on your concentration.
- 1, 8, 15, 16, 24, or 26, your reading and comprehension skills are holding you back.
- 3, 14, or 22, you need to learn the proper way to study for tests and how to reduce test anxiety.
- 4, 6, 10, 11, 13, 21, or 23, your organizational skills are letting you down.
- 7, 19, 27, you're spending a lot of time "writing" papers but haven't learned proper research or organizational skills.
- 9 or 28, you need to hone your computer skills.
- 12, 17, 20, or 25, you need a better system for taking notes in class and from your textbooks.

It is not as important how *many* "yes" answers you had as it is how many were grouped in a specific area—the one in which you obviously need help. (Though 10 or more yes answers should certainly indicate big problems in more than a single area.)

Let's go into a little more detail and get an even firmer handle on the current state of your study skills. I've listed the primary study skills on the next page. Take a separate piece of paper and rate yourself on each of them (from reading to test preparation) *before you read the rest of this chapter*. Then give yourself two points for every A, one point for every B, and zero points for every C.

If your overall rating is 18 or more, give yourself an A on the "Initial self-evaluation" line; 13 to 17, give yourself a B; and if 12 or less, give yourself a C. This is your assessment of your study habits as they exist right now.

Now let's review each of these areas, giving you insight as to what "excellent," "good," and "fair" really mean. As you read each section, fill in your rating on the "Your Starting Point" chart—and be honest with yourself. This evaluation will give you a benchmark from which to measure your improvement after you've completed the book. File it away and make the comparison when you've completed reading.

Remember: There are no right or wrong answers in either of these assessments. They are jumping-off points from which you can measure your progress and identify those areas in which your skills need improvement.

Your Starting Point

Initial self-evaluation	A ( )	B ( )	C ( )
Reading	A ( )	B ( )	C ( )
Memory development	A ( )	B ( )	C ( )
Time management	A ( )	B ( )	C ( )
Textbook note taking	A ( )	B ( )	C ( )
Classroom note taking	A ( )	B ( )	C ( )
Classroom participation	A ( )	B ( )	C ( )
Basic library skills	A ( )	B ( )	C ( )
Computer skills	A ( )	B ( )	C ( )
Library note taking	A ( )	B ( )	C ( )
Writing papers	A ( )	B ( )	C ( )
Test preparation	A ( )	B ( )	C ( )
Overall study skill level	A ( )	B ( )	C ( )

Reading

Speed, comprehension, and recall are the three important components of reading. Comprehension and recall are especially interrelated—better to sacrifice some speed to increase these two factors. To test your reading and comprehension skills, read the passage below (excerpted from *American Firsts* by Stephen Spignesi, New Page Books, 2004). Then close the book, jot down the key points made in the selection you read, review the text, and compare your notes with the reading selection. You will get a good idea of how well you understood what you read and just how good your "top-of-the-mind" recall is.

Bar codes are everywhere these days. They are automatically printed on almost every manufactured item—even though there are still many retail outlets that do not use bar code scanning devices. Someday, though, everyone will, the thinking goes, and so the code is printed on more than 95 percent of consumer items.

A bar code consists of 12 numbers separated by double lines at the beginning, middle, and end of the sequence. A laser/optical scanner reads the pattern of the numbers and instantly identifies the item and its correct price. Bar codes have been a boon to the retail industry, as well as the United States military, which requires that every single item it purchases have a scannable bar code. Bar codes allow speedy checkouts at stores, continual inventory updating, and accurate information about purchasing patterns.

Bar codes were invented in 1948 by Bernard Silver, a graduate student of Drexel Institute in Philadelphia, and Joseph Woodland, his partner. They initially worked with ultraviolet ink, but eventually settled on the pattern matching system in use today.

Some conspiracy theorists believe that the government eventually plans to have bar codes placed on every citizen, either on the back of the wrist or on the forehead, for constant monitoring of the populace. Interestingly, it was recently announced that laser bar code technology has advanced to the point where bar codes can now be imprinted directly onto meat and eggs and be read without damaging the product.

This means that, yes, bar codes can now safely be placed on human flesh. Imagine a future in which you order a ticket to a baseball game at home on the Internet using your own personal bar code ID number. When you get to the stadium, you hold out your hand, and an optical scanner reads the bar code tattooed (or whatever) on the back of your wrist. The master database (which everyone will be sharing by then) confirms that you did, indeed, purchase a ticket, and you get whisked through the entrance in the time it takes to swipe a bag of chips across a grocery store cash register scanner.

Science fiction? Not really. We're pretty close to this scenario already.

Score: If you can read the material straight through and accurately summarize what you've read, all in less than two minutes, give yourself an A. If you have some problems reading and understanding the text but are able to complete the assignment in less than four minutes, give yourself a B. If you are unable to complete the assignment in that time, remember what you read, or produce accurate notes at all, give yourself a C.

Retention

Test #1: Look at the number following this paragraph for 10 seconds. Then cover the page and write down as much of it as you can remember:

762049582049736

Score: If you remembered 12 or more digits in the correct order, give yourself an A; 8 to 11, a B; 7 or less, a C.

Test #2: Below are 12 nonsense words from a language I just made up and their "definitions." Study the list for 60 seconds and try to remember each word, how it's spelled, and its definition:

Berilly	excited	**Narouf**	bedpan
Simpoc	to cry	**Mccusker**	to dream
Delmak	old man	**Yerbtry**	salt
Triddle	to wade	**Armulla**	coffee cup
Gazdon	lion	**Frabje**	to skip
Cognit	spine	**Eklek**	lunch

Done? Close the book and write down each of the 12 words and its definition. They do not need to be in the order in which they were listed.

Score: If you accurately listed nine or more words and definitions (and that includes spelling my new words correctly), give yourself an A. If you listed from five to eight words and their definitions, or correctly listed and spelled nine or more words but mixed up their definitions, give yourself a B. If you were unable to remember at least four words and their definitions, give yourself a C.

Time Management

Your effective use of available study time can be measured by two yardsticks: (1) your ability to break down assignments into component parts (e.g., reading, note taking, outlining, writing); and (2) your ability to complete each task in an efficient manner.

Score: If you feel you use your time wisely and efficiently, give yourself an A. If you know there *are* times you simply run out of time, give yourself a B. If you can't *tell* time, give yourself a C.

Library Skills

Making the most of the library is a function of understanding its organization—and *using* it! The more time you spend there—studying, reading, researching—the more productive you'll be. You'll become adept at tracking down reference materials and finding the information you need quickly.

Virtually all libraries follow the same organization— once you understand it you'll be "library literate," no matter what library you use. In this book, you'll discover what kinds of resources are available (books, periodicals, directories, encyclopedias, dictionaries, magazines, newspapers, documents, microfilm files) and learn how to find materials using the Dewey decimal and Library of Congress Systems as well as the library's computerized system.

To better evaluate your library skills, answer the following questions:

1. What collections are restricted in your library?
2. Where would you find a biography of Herbert Hoover in your local library? Where is the reference section in your local library?
3. Given the Dewey number for a book, could you find it in less than five minutes? The Library of Congress number?
4. How often have you been to the library in the past six months? The past month?
5. Do you know how to find books, periodicals, and so forth using the library's computerized card catalog?

Score: If the answers to these questions are all obvious to you, indicating a steady pattern of library use, then you can claim to have the library habit—give yourself an A. If you're unable to answer at least four of the questions or will freely own up to a spotty record of library use, give yourself a B. If you don't have the faintest clue of where the closest library is, give yourself a C.

Computer Skills

It's virtually impossible now to succeed at almost any level of education without complete mastery of the computer. But knowing how
to use a computer is just the beginning. You have to know how to use
it to study more efficiently and more effectively. That includes learning how to write better papers, keep your schedules, and taking
advantage of the almost limitless research possibilities available online.

Score: If you are capable of doing just about anything online short of
hacking the Pentagon, and have made your computer equipment a
key tool in your quest for more efficient studying and better grades,
give yourself an A. If you are adept at word processing and playing
games and at least can get online, but have never used 75 percent of
the other tools on your computer and "wipe out" more often than
surf, give yourself a B. If you don't even know what "being online"
means and need four minutes to figure out how to turn your computer on, give yourself a C.

Note Taking

Different arenas—at home with your textbooks, in the classroom, at
the library, and online—require different methods of note taking.

From your textbooks: Working from your textbooks, you should
identify the main ideas, rephrase information in your own words, as
well as capture the details with which you were unfamiliar. Take brief,
concise notes in a separate notebook as you read. You should write
down questions and answers to ensure your mastery of the material,
starring those questions for which you *don't* have answers so you can
ask them in class.

In class: Class *preparation* is the key to class *participation*. By reading material to be covered before class, you will be able to concentrate
and absorb the teacher's interpretations and points. Using a topical,
short sentence approach or your own shorthand or symbols, take
notes on those items that will trigger thematic comprehension of the

subject matter. Your notes should be sequential, following the teacher's lecture pattern. Review your notes at the first opportunity following class. Fill in any blanks and add your own thoughts.

In the library or online: What's the difference between taking notes at the library or working at home with library books or those you've found online vs. your own textbooks? Sooner or later you'll have to return library books (if you're allowed to take them out at all), and librarians tend to frown on highlighting them. And unless you plan to print out every Web page you find and wield your magic highlighter, you need an effective system for taking notes right from the source, whether it's a library book or Web page.

Score: Are your note-taking skills sufficient to summarize the necessary data from your textbooks and capture the key points from classroom lectures and discussions? Do they allow you to get the information you need from a variety of sources, prepare detailed outlines, and write good papers? Give yourself an A. If you feel you are deficient in any one of these, give yourself a B. If notes are what you pass to your friends in class, give yourself a C.

Class Participation

Most teachers take each student's class participation into account when giving grades, no matter how many pop quizzes they pull or how many term papers they assign. And, you may have discovered, there are teachers out there who will mark down even those students who "ace" every paper and quiz if they seem to disappear in the classroom.

Score: If you are always prepared for class (which means, at the very least, reading all assigned material, preparing assigned homework and projects, and turning them in on time), actively participate in discussions, and ask frequent and pertinent questions as a way of both trumpeting what you already know and filling in the gaps in that knowledge, give yourself an A. If you fail in any of these criteria, give yourself a B. If you aren't sure where the classroom is, give yourself a C.

Writing Paper and Preparing Oral Reports

Preparing any sort of report, written or oral, is 90 percent perspiration (research) and 10 percent inspiration (writing). In other words, the ability to write a good paper is more dependent on your mastery of the other skills we've already discussed than your mastery of *writing*. If you are an avid reader, familiar with your local library, a veteran online researcher, a good note taker, and capable of breaking down the most complex topic into the manageable steps necessary to write a paper, you probably turn in superior papers.

Score: If you have already given yourself an A in library skills, library and online note taking, time management, and reading, give yourself an A. If you feel you turn in relatively good papers but definitely lack in any of these areas, give yourself a B. If your idea of writing a paper is photocopying the pertinent *Cliffs Notes* and recopying the summary in your own handwriting, give yourself a C.

Test Preparation

The key to proper test preparation is knowing what material will be covered and what form the test will take. Weekly quizzes or unit/chapter exams usually cover the most recent material. Midterms and finals cover a much broader area—usually all the subject matter to date. Multiple-choice tests, essays, lists of math problems, and science lab tests all require different preparation and apply different test-taking skills. Knowing the kind of test you're facing will make your preparation much easier.

So will creating a list of questions you think your teacher will most likely ask. By periodically reviewing your text and class notes, you'll begin to identify the areas in which your teacher appears most interested … and on which he or she is most likely to test you. As a final trick, prepare a list of 10 or more questions *you* would ask if *you* were the teacher.

Score: If you are able to construct tests that are harder than the ones your teacher gives you—and score well on his or hers—give yourself an A. If you feel you know the material, but somehow don't perform as well as you think you should at test time, give yourself a B. If you didn't pass your driver's test, let alone algebra, give yourself a C.

Your Overall Score

Once again, after you've rated yourself in each area, give yourself two points for every A, one point for every B, and zero points for every C. If your overall rating is 18 or more, excellent (give yourself an A); 13 to 17, good (give yourself a B); 12 or less, fair (give yourself a C). Put your new score in the line "Overall study skill level" in the "Your Starting Point" chart on page 5.

How closely did this more detailed evaluation compare with the score you gave yourself before reading the rest of this chapter? If the latter was wildly off the mark, it just means you aren't as ready to toss this book as you wanted to be! If your initial evaluation wasn't as positive as the more detailed one you just completed, you're in better shape than you thought!

Now What?

The fact that you have been honest with yourself in evaluating the talents you bring to the study game is a big plus in your favor. Knowing where you are strong and where you need to improve makes everything else a good deal easier. Now, based on your test results, draw up a list of your assets and liabilities—your areas of strength and weakness. This will focus your attention on those areas that require the most work to improve.

While I would strongly recommend you read the entire book, this simple test has enabled you to identify the chapters you really need to study and the specific skills that may require your continued attention long after you finish reading this book.

CHAPTER 2

HOW TO ORGANIZE YOUR STUDYING

W hat effect can good study habits have? I suspect native-born talents and skills—the basic abilities you're born with—have the most to do with success in school—50 percent, maybe even 60. And the environment in which you're trying to learn, your health, and other such factors may account for another 10 percent, maybe 15. That leaves 25 to 40 percent for study skills.

Don't believe that learning how to study can have such a monstrous effect? First, read *How to Study*, practice the skills, and watch the results. I think you'll discover I'm right. Second, if you don't believe study skills are so important, you must believe something like "smart kids do well because they're smart." Well, a lot of smart kids *don't* do well. At *all*. Others do well in school but test poorly. And many are great in some subjects and not so great in others. I don't have to prove this. Look at your friends, at others in your school. I guarantee you'll prove it to yourself.

What kind of effort are we talking about here? Another hour a night? Two hours a night? *More*? And what about that "study smarter, not harder" slogan that's associated with my *How to Study Program*? "If I'm studying longer," you might reasonably contend, "I'm sure as heck studying harder, at least by my definition."

Let's take the latter point first. You *can* study smarter. You *can* put in less time and get better results. But learning how to do so *is* hard, because learning of *any* kind takes discipline. And learning self-discipline is, to many of us, the most difficult task of all. So don't kid yourself: You aren't going to sit down, skim *How to Study,* and miraculously transform yourself from a C student to an A student. But you absolutely can achieve such results if you put in the time to learn the lessons this book contains and, more importantly, practice and use them every day.

If you're currently doing little or nothing in the way of schoolwork, then you *are* going to have to put in more time and effort. How much more? Or even more generally, how long should you study? Until you get the results you want to achieve. The smarter you are and the more easily you learn and adapt the techniques in *How to Study,* the more likely you will spend *less* time on your homework than before. But the further you need to go—from Ds to As rather than Bs to As—the more you need to learn and the longer you need to give yourself to learn it.

Don't get discouraged. You *will* see positive results surprisingly quickly.

Make Study Habit-Forming

If you're doing poorly in school even while putting in a reasonable amount of study time, you've got poor study habits. Who knows where or when you acquired them, but failure has, to some extent, become a habit.

Good news! Not only can *bad* habits be broken, but they can be replaced by *good* habits relatively easily. Here's your battle plan:

- It is much easier to *replace* a habit than to break it entirely. So don't attempt to stop poor study habits— just learn the good ones to substitute for them.
- Practice, practice, practice. Practice is the motor oil that lubricates any habit's engine. The more you do something, the more ingrained it becomes.

- Tell your friends and family of your decision to improve your study skills and do better in school. (This is a trick that works for *some* people, who find that the added pressure is a good motivator.)

- For others, however, such a strategy simply adds *too much* pressure and is more likely to backfire instead, encouraging *failure*. My advice would be to use such a strategy if you know it will help you, but avoid it if you know it will actually hurt.

- You don't have to grind it out from Ds to As with no feedback. To make sure you get a "motivational jolt" from every accomplishment, resolve to chart every inch of your progress, even if, like Robert Frost, you have "miles to go before you sleep." You may want to set up a chart on your wall on which you list "Today's Successes" *every day*. And remember the small steps you're taking—saving five minutes on a reading assignment, finding the books you need at the library more quickly, feeling that you took good notes in a lecture, raising your hand to actually answer a professor's question in a class discussion, and so on.

Starting with the next chapter, everything in this book will concentrate on specific strategies useful for specific tasks—paper writing, note taking, test taking, reading, and so forth. So this is probably the best place to discuss some overall study strategies that have little to do with any particular task but everything to do with your eventual study success.

Get Ready to Become a "Lifer"

Learning how to study is really a long-term process. Once you undertake the journey, you will be surprised at the number of landmarks, pathways, side streets, and road signs you'll find. Even after you've transformed yourself into a better student than you'd ever hoped to be, you'll inevitably find one more signpost that offers new information, one more pathway that leads you in an interesting new direction.

Consider learning how to study a *lifelong process*, and be ready to modify anything you're doing as you learn other methods.

This is especially important right from the start, when you consider your overall study strategies. How long should you study per night? How do you allocate time between subjects? How often should you schedule breaks? Your answers to these questions are going to vary considerably depending on how well you were doing *before* you read this book, how far you have to go, how interested you are in getting there, how involved you are in other activities, the time of day, your general health, and a host of other individual factors.

What's your study sequence? Hardest assignments first? Easiest? Longest? Shortest? Are you comfortable switching back and forth from one to another, or do you prefer to focus on a single assignment from start to finish?

What's your study strategy? Your high school history teacher may want you to memorize a series of battles, dates, and generals. Your college professor will expect a deeper understanding of the battles, how they related to the overall conduct of the war, and how they affected or were affected by what was occurring in the rest of the world. *Your teacher's emphasis will change the way you study.*

This gets even more difficult (believe it or not!) when you consider that the tasks themselves may have a great effect on your schedule. When I sit down to plan out the chapter of a book, for example, I need a relatively long period of uninterrupted time—at least an hour, perhaps as long as three hours. That enables me to put my notes in the order I want them and think through the entire chapter—writing transitions in my head, noting problem areas, figuring out where I need an example or illustration. If I only have half an hour before a meeting or appointment, I wouldn't even attempt to start such a project.

What's the lesson in all of this? There is no ideal, no answer— certainly no "right" answer—to many of the questions I've posed. It's a message you'll read in these pages again and again: Figure out what works for you and keep on doing it. If it later stops working or doesn't seem to be working as well, change it.

None of the study techniques discussed at length in this book is carved in stone. Not only should you feel free to adapt and shape and bend them to your own needs, you *must* do so.

When Teachers Rule

A key way to do better on any test is to read the instructions before you start it. This helps you avoid the poor grade (not to mention the frustration and embarrassment) that results from trying to answer all six essay questions in an hour when you were only supposed to pick three.

Tests aren't the only time "reading the instructions" is important. Many teachers have their own rules and regulations about turning in homework assignments, preparing papers or projects, reporting lab results, etc. And it's just as important to follow *their* instructions— and just as devastating if you *don't*.

I really did have a teacher in 10th grade—when none of us had access to personal computers and few of us had learned to type—who failed a student because her paper was handwritten. What bothered me then was that the paper was really *good…and* it didn't mean a hill of beans to that teacher. The farther along you are in school, the less likely your instructors will cut you any slack.

Be Proud of Your Work . . . And Show It

Do you know someone who makes sure he counts every word of a 500-word assignment and heads to a conclusion as soon as he approaches that magic number?

How about the student who is convinced her chicken scratch is perfectly decipherable, even when the teacher has to wade through several crossouts on every page and follow arrows from one page to another? Or the one who only spells one thing correctly per paper— his name—or, even worse, spells a word correctly two or three times and incorrectly four or five others…all on the same page?

Teachers are human. They respond to presentation. If the *substance* of two papers or tests or projects is relatively equal, the *form* in which they're presented may well affect the grade, perhaps significantly.

Besides, there are a lot of teachers who make it a point to decrease grades because of poor grammar, spelling, or overall presentation. Just as there are others who may subconsciously give a better grade to a paper that clearly shows a student cares.

Know Thy Teachers

Teachers are different, too, in their approach to their subjects, as well as their expectations, standards, flexibility, and so on. It certainly is worth the effort to compile a "profile" of each of your teachers. What do each of them want to see in terms of notes, level of participation, papers, projects? What are their individual likes and dislikes? Their methods of grading and testing?

Knowing these various traits should certainly lead you to approach each class—and each teacher—differently. Let's say—not that it would ever *really* happen to *you*, of course—that you have managed to dig yourself a very deep hole. It's 11 p.m., you're well past your study prime, and you still have reading assignments to complete for English and history tomorrow morning.

Your English teacher demands maximum class participation and makes it a large part of your grade—and test scores be damned. Her hobby seems to be calling on the unprepared, and she has an uncanny and unerring knack for ferreting those students out.

Your history teacher discourages discussion, preferring to lecture and answer a couple of questions at the end of the class. He never calls on anyone for anything.

Given this situation, and knowing you can stay awake long enough to read only one of the two assignments, which would you pick? Would there ever be a time, barring a simultaneous typhoon, eclipse, and national holiday, that you would show up for that English class unprepared?

While I'll show you in Chapter 4 how to ensure that poor scheduling does not become a habit that dooms you to such choices, I suspect that far too many of you do not take the natural differences among your teachers into account when scheduling homework, preparing papers, or studying for tests.

Likewise, I suspect that far too few of you try to create a bond with one special teacher—a mentoring relationship— that could help you avoid some of the bumps and swerves and reach your goal with far less trouble. Why should you go out of your way to find a mentor? Because you probably need more help—in life, not just in school— than your friends or parents can provide. A mentor can give you that perspective, advice, and help.

Intrinsic and Extrinsic Motivation

Motivators are either intrinsic or extrinsic. What's the difference? You sign up for a voice class. While the hours certainly apply to your graduating requirements, you attend class because you love singing.

You also signed up for biology. You hate the thought of dissecting frogs, and you couldn't care less whether they have exoskeletons, endoskeletons, hydroskeletons, or no skeletons at all, but the class is required.

In the first case, you're motivated by intrinsic factors— you are taking the voice class simply because you truly enjoy it.

The second scenario is an example of *extrinsic* motivation. While you have no interest in biology, your reward for taking the class is external—you'll be able to graduate.

Extrinsic motivation can help you make it through boring or unpleasant tasks that are part of the process of reaching your goals. A vivid image of your final goal can be a powerful motivating force. One student thought about what his job as a computer programmer would be like whenever he needed some help getting through class.

Try imagining a day in *your* life 5 or 10 years from now. If you can't, no *wonder* you're having a hard time motivating yourself to work toward that career as a final goal!

A specific role model may also be an effective motivator. When she was a first grader, my daughter Lindsay became particularly enamored of Wilma Rudolph. Growing up black and poor was a minor part of Wilma's childhood problems. When she contracted polio, doctors told her she would never walk again. My daughter thought it was amazing that Wilma, through sheer guts and determination, not only walked again but became the fastest woman in the world, winning multiple Olympic gold medals. When confronted with her own (smaller!) problems, my daughter still reminds herself that "If Wilma could do it, I can, too." What a great way to motivate yourself! Think of your own role models in life. And if you don't have any, find some!

The Goal Pyramid

One way to visualize all your goals—and their relationship to each other—is to construct what I call a *goal pyramid*. Here's how to do it:

1. Centered at the top of a piece of paper, write down where you hope to be—and what you want to be doing—3, 5, or 10 years from now. This is your long-range goal and the pinnacle of your pyramid.

2. Below your long-range goal(s), list mid-range goals— milestones or steps that will lead you to your eventual target.

3. Below the mid-range goals, list as many short-range goals as you can—smaller steps that can be completed in relatively short periods of time.

Change your goal pyramid as you progress through school. You may eventually decide on a different career. Or your mid-range goals may change as you decide on a different path leading to the long-range goal. The short-range goals will undoubtedly change, even daily.

The process of creating your own goal pyramid allows you to see *how* all those little daily and weekly steps you take can lead to your mid-range and long-term goals, and will thereby motivate you to work on your daily and weekly tasks with more energy and enthusiasm.

The development of good study skills is the highway to your goals, whatever they are. No matter how hard you have to work or how much adversity you have to overcome along the way, the journey will indeed be worth it.

How do you make setting goals a part of your life? Here are some hints I think will help:

- **Be realistic when you set goals.** Don't aim too high or too low, and don't be particularly concerned when (not *if*) you have to make adjustments along the way.

- **Be realistic about your expectations.** Seek a greater understanding of a subject for which you have little aptitude rather than getting hopelessly bogged down if total mastery is just not in the cards.

- **Don't give up too easily.** You can be *overly* realistic— too ready to give up just because something is a trifle harder than you'd like. Don't aim too high and feel miserable when you don't come close, or aim too low and never achieve your potential—find the path that's right for you.

- **Concentrate on areas that offer the best chance for improvement.** Unexpected successes can do wonders for your confidence and might make it possible for you to achieve more than you thought you could, even in other areas.

- **Monitor your achievements and keep resetting your goals.** Daily, weekly, monthly, yearly—ask yourself how you've done and where you'd like to go *now*.
- **Put your goal pyramid right up on the wall.** See it. Feel it. Live it.

Use Rewards as Artificial Motivators

The way you decide to use a reward system depends on how much help you need getting motivated to study. As we've observed, tasks that are intrinsically interesting require little outside motivation. However, most schoolwork can be spurred along by the promise of little rewards along the way. If the task is especially tedious or difficult, make the rewards more frequent so that your energy and determination don't flag.

As a general rule, the size of the reward should match the difficulty of the task. For an hour of reading, promise yourself a 15-minute ice-cream break. When you complete a rough draft for a big assignment, treat yourself to a movie.

Three Great Ways to Get Super Organized

As you begin to make goal setting and organization a part of your daily life, here are three concepts that will make a huge difference in your success.

Small Changes Add Up to Big Results

A simple, tiny change in your behavior may have virtually negligible results, but make *hundreds* of small changes, and the effects can be earth-shattering!

Make this rule become an automatic part of your thought process and your actions. It will help you understand the often small difference between success and failure, productivity and frustration, happiness and agony. It's so simple, it's deceptive. What is the key to *your* success? Maybe just a little more training. Maybe a slightly better method of planning. Maybe just overcoming one tiny bad habit. Maybe all of these and more. Each change alone may be almost inconsequential, but when added up, a host of small changes can lead to incredible results!

The 80–20 Rule (The Pareto Principle)

Another rule that you can apply to make a difference in how well you organize and manage your priorities is the 80–20 Rule, also known as the Pareto Principle.

Victor Pareto was an Italian economist and sociologist at the turn of the 20th century who studied land ownership in Italy. Pareto discovered that more than 80 percent of the land was owned by less than 20 percent of the people. As he studied other things that people owned (including money), he found the same principle held true:

20 percent or less of the people always ended up with 80 percent or more of whatever he measured.

The most astonishing revelation about the 80–20 Rule is its corollary: If 20 percent of activities are producing 80 percent of the results, then the other 80 percent of activities are only producing 20 percent.

Remember: To apply the 80-20 Rule to managing your priorities, remind yourself that 20 percent of the activities on your list are going to produce 80 percent of the results and payoff. Your question must constantly be, "Which activities are part of the 20 percent?"

But don't get too hung up on statistics, especially misleading ones. An ex-partner of mine once noticed that 45 percent of the books published one year made most of the profits, so he instructed everyone to just publish the 45 percent of books *next* year that would make money. Think about it.

Take Advantage of "In-between" Time

You can be even more productive by identifying the little windows of opportunity that open every day. They don't arrive with much fanfare, so if you're not alert to them, you'll never even notice them. What must you do with this "inbetween" time, while you're stuck in traffic, waiting in line, or sitting by the phone? Recognize it as soon as it occurs and utilize it immediately by taking premeditated action. If you don't have a plan, you will waste this time!

Here are some suggestions:

- Make phone calls.
- Read something.
- Mail letters.
- Pick up groceries (or make your grocery list).
- Clean your desk and return things to their proper places.
- Review your daily schedule and reprioritize, if necessary.
- Go through your mail.
- Write a quick note or letter home.
- Proofread some or all of one of your papers.
- Think! (About an upcoming assignment, a paper you're writing, any upcoming project.)
- Relax!

How Perfect Are You?

Superior students show they care about their work and consistently apply the effort necessary to achieve their goals. Perfectionists care perhaps *too* much, finding it impossible to be satisfied with anything less than "perfect" work (as they define it), presuming for a moment that such an ideal can actually be attained.

It is possible, of course, to score a "perfect" 100 on a test or to get an A+ on a paper the teacher calls "Perfect!" in the margin. But in reality, doing anything "perfectly" is an impossible task.

What does all this have to do with you? Nothing, unless you find yourself spending two hours polishing what is already an A+ paper or half an hour searching for that one "perfect" word or an hour rewriting great notes to make them "absolutely perfect." In other words, while striving for perfection may well be a noble trait, it can easily, perhaps inevitably, become an uncontrollable and unstoppable urge that seriously inhibits your enjoyment of your work and your life.

If you find yourself fighting this demon, remind yourself (frequently) of the Law of Diminishing Returns: Your initial effort yields the biggest results, with each succeeding effort yielding proportionately less. And there comes a point where even the most *prodigious* efforts yield *negligible* results. This applies not only to perfectionists, but also to those of you who scoff at the very thought of using a "simple" outline or producing a "formulaic" report. You do not have to always be innovative, dazzling, and creative. You do not have to invent a new, multimedia, interactive book report. Sometimes a good six-page book report that gets an A– is just fine, and that A+ "innovation" is more trouble (and time!) than it's worth!

When I am tempted to do far more than necessary, just because it would be a "cool" solution (and time consuming and wasteful and inefficient and difficult), I think of George Simenon, the French author best known for his Inspector Maigret mystery series—and the 500 total books he wrote in his lifetime. How did he do it... and still have time to eat and sleep? Simple—he used only 2,000 vocabulary words (out of the 800,000 plus available to him) so he wouldn't have to interrupt his writing to consult a dictionary or thesaurus. (And he probably *didn't* eat or sleep much.)

If you really would prefer spending another couple of hours polishing that A+ paper or searching for a website your teacher's never heard of to taking in a movie, reading a book, or getting some *other* assignment done, be my guest. Is the extra effort *really* worth it? Maybe in some cases, but not usually.

Creating Your Study Environment

I have included a checklist below for you to rate your study environment. It includes not just *where* you study, but *when* and *how* you study, too. Once you've identified what works for you, avoid those situations in which you *know* you don't perform best. If you don't know the answer to one or more of the questions, take the time to experiment.

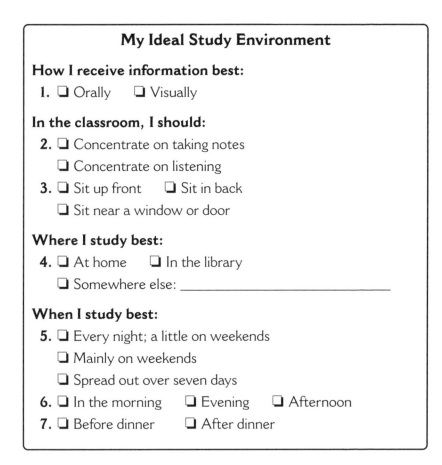

My Ideal Study Environment

How I receive information best:
1. ❑ Orally   ❑ Visually

In the classroom, I should:
2. ❑ Concentrate on taking notes
   ❑ Concentrate on listening
3. ❑ Sit up front   ❑ Sit in back
   ❑ Sit near a window or door

Where I study best:
4. ❑ At home   ❑ In the library
   ❑ Somewhere else: _____

When I study best:
5. ❑ Every night; a little on weekends
   ❑ Mainly on weekends
   ❑ Spread out over seven days
6. ❑ In the morning   ❑ Evening   ❑ Afternoon
7. ❑ Before dinner   ❑ After dinner

How I study best:

8. ❑ Alone   ❑ With a friend   ❑ In a group

9. ❑ Under time pressure
   ❑ Before I know I have to

10. ❑ With music   ❑ In front of the TV
    ❑ In a quiet room

11. ❑ Organizing an entire night's studying before I start
    ❑ Tackling and completing one subject at a time

I need to take a break:

12. ❑ Every 30 minutes or so   ❑ Every hour
    ❑ Every 2 hours   ❑ Every _____ hours

Many of the items on this chart should be understandable to you now. *Why* you feel the need for a particular environment is not important. Knowing you *have a preference* is. Here's what you're trying to assess in each item of the checklist:

1. If you prefer "listening" to "seeing," you'll have little problem getting the information you need from class lectures and discussions. In fact, you'll *prefer* them to studying your textbooks. (You may have to concentrate on your reading skills and spend more time with your textbooks to offset this tendency. Highlighting your texts may help.)

   If you're more of a "visual" person, you'll probably find it easier reading your textbook and may have to work to improve your classroom concentration. Taking excellent class notes that you can read later will probably be important for you. You'll also want to adapt your note-taking methods to your visual preference: Rather than writing notes like everybody else, draw pictures, use charts, and learn how to "map" a lecture.

2. This should tie in with your answer to (I). The more "aural" you are, the more you should concentrate on listening. The more "visual," the better your notes should be for later review.

3. This may make a difference for a number of reasons. You may find it difficult to hear or see from the back of the classroom. You may be shy and want to sit up front to motivate yourself to participate in class discussions. You may find sitting near a window makes you feel a little less claustrophobic; alternatively, you may daydream too much if you are near a window and should sit as far "inside" the classroom as possible.

4. Whatever location you find most conducive to study (considering the limitations of your current living situation and schedule) should be where you spend most of your study time.

5. Deciding how to organize your time to most effectively cover the material may depend, in part, on the amount of homework you are burdened with and/or the time of year. You may have one schedule during most of the school year but have to adapt during test time, when papers are due, for special projects, etc.

6. To some of you, such preferences may only be a factor on weekends, because your day hours are set—you're in school.

But if you're in college (or in a high school program that mimics college's "choose your own courses and times" scheduling procedures), you would want to use this factor in determining when to schedule your classes.

If you study best in the morning, for example, try to schedule as many classes as possible in the afternoons (or, at worst, late in the morning).

If you study best in the evening, either schedule morning classes and leave your afternoons free for other activities, or schedule them in the afternoons so you can sleep later (and study later the night before).

7. Some of us get cranky if we try to do anything when we're hungry. If you study poorly when your stomach is growling, eat something!

8. Most of us grow up automatically studying alone. If we study with a friend, there's often more talking, TV watching, anything but studying. But don't underestimate the positive effect studying with one or two friends—or even a larger study group—can have on your mastery of schoolwork and your grades. (I discuss study groups in greater detail at the end of this section.)

9. Just because you perform best under pressure doesn't mean you should always leave projects, papers, and studying for tests until the last minute. It just means you won't panic when an unexpected project gets assigned or a surprise test is announced.

   If you do not study well under pressure, it certainly doesn't mean you occasionally won't be required to do so. The better organized you are, the easier it will be for you to avoid panicking when the unexpected arises.

10. As we've discussed, some of you (like me) will find it difficult to concentrate without music or some sort of noise. Others couldn't sit in front of the TV and do anything but breathe and eat.

    Many of you will fall in between—you can read and even take notes to music but need absolute quiet to study for a test or master particularly difficult concepts. If you don't know how you function best, now is the time to find out.

11. Choosing the second option—starting and finishing one project before moving on to another—doesn't mean you can't at least sit down and outline an entire night's study plan before tackling each subject, one at a time. Setting up such a study schedule is advised. But it may mean you really can't move to another project while the first one is unfinished. Other people may have no problem working on one project, switching to another when they get stuck or just need a break, then going back to the first.

12. There's nothing particularly wrong with taking a break whenever you feel you need to keep yourself sharp and maximize your quality study time—as long as the breaks aren't every five minutes and don't last longer than the study periods! In general, though, try to increase your concentration through practice so that you can go at least an hour before getting up, stretching, and having a drink or snack. Too many projects will require at least that long to "get into" or organize, and you may find that breaking too frequently will require too much "review time" when you return to your desk.

Study Groups: What Are Friends For?

I never got invited to join a study group while I was in college and didn't think of forming one myself. If I had thought of it, even while I was in high school, I would have probably started one.

The idea is simple: Find a small group of like-minded students and share notes, question each other, and prepare for tests together. To be effective, obviously, the students you pick should share all, or at least most, of your classes.

Search out students who are smarter than you, but not too much smarter. If they are on a level far beyond your own, you'll soon be left in the dust and be more discouraged than ever. On the other hand, if you choose students who are too far beneath your level, you may enjoy being the "brain" of the bunch but miss the point of the group— the challenge of other minds to spur you on.

Study groups can be organized in a variety of ways. Each member could be assigned primary responsibility for a single class, such as preparing detailed notes from lectures and discussion groups. If supplementary reading is recommended but not required, that person could be responsible for doing all such reading and preparing detailed summaries.

Alternatively, everybody can be responsible for his or her own notes, but the group could act as an ad hoc discussion group, refining understanding of key points, working on problems together, questioning each other, practicing for tests, and so forth.

Even if you find only one or two other students willing to work with you, such cooperation will be invaluable, especially in preparing for major exams.

Tips for Forming Your Own Study Group

- I suggest four students minimum, probably six maximum. You want to ensure everyone gets a chance to participate as much as he or she wants while maximizing the collective knowledge and wisdom of the group.

- While group members needn't be best friends, they shouldn't be overtly hostile to one another, either. Seek diversity of experience and demand common dedication.

- Try to select students who are at least as smart, committed, and serious as you. That will encourage you to keep up and challenge you a bit. Avoid a group in which you're the "star"— at least until you flicker out during the first exam.

- Avoid inviting members who are inherently unequal into the group—boyfriend/girlfriend combinations, in which one or the other may be inhibited by their amore's presence; situations where one student works for another; situations where underclassmen and upperclassmen may stifle one another—you get the idea.

- Decide early on if you're forming a study group or a social group. If it's the latter, don't pretend it's the former. If the former, don't just invite your friends and informally sit around discussing your teachers for an hour each week.

- My suggestion is to assign each class to one student. Each student must master his or her assigned class, completing any supplemental assigned reading, taking outstanding notes, outlining the course (if the group so desires), being available for questions, and preparing various practice quizzes, midterms, and finals as needed.

  Needless to say, all of the other students should still attend class, take their own notes, and do their own reading and homework assignments. But the student assigned a particular class should attempt to actually become the "substitute professor" of that class in the study group.

  So if you have five classes, a five-person study group is ideal.

- Make meeting times and assignments formal and rigorous. Consider establishing rigid rules of conduct. Better to shake out the nonserious students early. You don't want anyone who wants to work as little as possible to take advantage of your hard work.

- Consider appointing a chair in charge of keeping everyone to schedule and settling disputes before they disrupt the study group.

- However you organize, clearly decide—early—the exact requirements and assignments of each student. Again, you never want the feeling to emerge that one or two of you are trying to "ride the coattails" of the others.

Where Should You Study?

- **At the library.** There may be numerous choices, from the large reading room to quieter, sometimes deserted, specialty rooms to your own study cubicle. My favorite "home away from home" at Princeton was a little room that seemingly only four or five of us knew about—with wonderfully comfortable chairs, subdued lighting, phonographs with earplugs, and a selection of some 500 classical records. For someone who needed music to study, it was custom made!

- **At home.** Remember that this is the place where distractions are most likely to occur. No one tends to telephone you at the library and little brothers (or your own kids) will not find you easily among the stacks of books. While home is usually the most convenient place to make your study headquarters, it may not be the most effective.

- **At a friend's, neighbor's, or relative's house.** This may not be an option for most of you, even on an occasional basis, but you may want to set up one or two alternative study sites. Despite many experts' opinions that you must study in the same place every night (with which I don't agree), I had a friend who simply craved some variety to help motivate him. He had four different places he liked to study and rotated them from night to night. Do whatever works for you.

- **In an empty classroom.** Certainly an option at many colleges and perhaps some private high schools, it is an interesting idea mainly because so few students have ever thought of it! While not a likely option at a public high school, it never hurts to ask if you can't make some arrangements. Since many athletic teams practice until 6 p.m. or later, even on the high school level, there may be a part of the school open—and usable with permission— even if the rest is locked up tight.

- **At your job.** Whether you're a student working part-time or a full-time worker going to school part-time, you may well be able to make arrangements to use an empty office, even during regular office hours, or perhaps after everyone has left (depending on how much your boss trusts you). If you're in middle or high school and a parent, friend, or relative works nearby, you may be able to work from just after school ends until closing time at his or her workplace.

Whatever place you choose for your study area, make it somewhere that is only for study. Which leaves out your bed, in front of the TV, and the dining room table, among other bad choices.

Just as you (hopefully) sit right down and go to work when you enter a classroom (presuming the teacher is in the room!), your attitude and attention will be automatic if you associate your study area solely with homework, not sleeping, eating, or entertaining yourself. And that will make the time you spend more effective and efficient.

When Should You Study?

As much as possible, create a routine time of day for your studying. Some experts contend that doing the same thing at the same time every day is the most effective way to organize any ongoing task. Some students find it easier to set aside specific blocks of time during the day, each day, in which they plan on studying.

No matter who you are, the time of day you'll study is determined by these factors:

- **Study when you're at your best.** What is your peak performance period—the time of day you do your best work? This period varies from person to person—you may be dead to the world until noon but able to study well into the night, or up and alert at the crack of dawn but distracted and tired if you try to burn the midnight oil. Just remember, focus = efficiency.

- **Consider your sleep habits.** Habit is a very powerful influence. If you always set your alarm for 7 a.m., you may soon start waking up just before the alarm goes off. If you have grown accustomed to going to sleep around 11 p.m., you will undoubtedly become quite tired if you try to study until 2 a.m., and probably accomplish very little during those three extra hours.

- **Study when you can.** Although you want to sit down to study when you are mentally most alert, external factors also play a role in deciding when you study. Being at your best is a great goal, but is not always possible. Study whenever circumstances allow.

- **Consider the complexity of the assignment when you allocate time.** The tasks themselves may have a great effect on your schedule. Don't schedule one hour for an 80-page reading assignment when you know you read half a page per minute...on a good day.

- **Use "nonprime" hours for the easiest tasks.** When your energy and motivation are at their lowest levels, should you really bore in on that project that's been giving you fits? Or merely recopy some notes, go over your calendar, or proofread a paper? When you're least creative, least energetic, and least motivated, why would you even consider tackling your most challenging assignments? Don't be like many businesspeople I know who schedule their time backwards: In the morning, when they're raring to go, they read the paper, check their email, and skim trade journals. At the end of the day, when they can barely see straight, they start on the presentation for the Board of Directors' meeting...tomorrow's Board of Directors' meeting.

- **Schedule study time immediately after class or, if that's not possible, immediately before.** This is most pertinent for college and graduate students, who may have significant free time between classes. Your memory of a class is, not surprisingly, strongest immediately after it, so allocating an open hour after class to go over notes, think about the lecture, and complete that day's assignment is the best way to spend that hour.

If that isn't possible, then taking the time to study immediately *before* class is an excellent second option, especially if you usually need that time to complete your assignments!

Evaluate Your Study Area

Whatever location you choose as your study base, how you set up your study area can affect your ability to stay focused and, if you aren't careful, seriously inhibit quality study time. Sit down at your desk or study area right now and evaluate your own study environment:

- Do you have one or two special places reserved just for studying? Or do you study wherever seems convenient or available at the time?

- Is your study area a pleasant place? Would you tout it to a friend as a good place to study? Or do you dread it because it's so depressing?

- How's the lighting? Is it too dim or too bright? Is the entire desk area well lit?

- Are all the materials you need handy?

- What else do you do here? Do you eat? Sleep? Write letters? Read for pleasure? If you try to study at the same place you sit to listen to music or chat on the phone, you may find yourself doing one when you think you're doing the other!

- Is your study area in a high-traffic area? How often are you interrupted by people passing through?

- Can you close the door to the room to avoid disturbances and outside noise?

- When do you spend the most time here? What time of day do you study? Is it when you are at your best? Or do you inevitably study when you're tired and less productive?

- Are your files, folders, and other class materials organized and near the work area? Do you have an effective filing system in place for them?

Set up a "future" drawer in your filing cabinet. When you find ideas, research material, and so on (from magazines, books, newspapers, websites, whatever) that you think may be important *sometime in the future*, write a pertinent note to yourself and file it. The time you take now will be a mere fraction of the time you save in the future.

Staying Focused on Your Studies

If you find yourself doodling and dawdling more than reading and remembering, try these solutions:

- **Create a work environment in which you're comfortable.** The size, style, and placement of your desk, chair, and lighting may all affect whether or not you're distracted from the work at hand. Take the time to design the area that's perfect for you. Needless to say, anything that you know will distract you—a girlfriend's picture, a radio or TV, whatever, should disappear from your study area.

- **Turn up the lights.** Experiment with the placement and intensity of lighting in your study area until you find what works for you, both in terms of comfort and as a means of staying awake and focused.

- **Set some rules.** Let family, relatives, and especially friends know how important your studying is and that designated study hours are inviolate.

- **Take the breaks you need.** Don't just follow well-intentioned but bogus advice about how long you should study before taking a break. Break when *you* need to.

- **Select a study symbol.** Choose something you can associate with studying, such as a hat, a scarf, even one of those little trolls people keep on their desks. Whenever it's time to study, just jam on the hat, wrap yourself in the scarf, or set the troll prominently on your desk. It's study time! Not only will this "get you in the mood" to study, it will serve as a warning to roommates, friends, or family members that you are working.

  Don't associate your new "study symbol" with anything *but* studying. Don't wear your study hat to baseball games or leave your troll on the desk while you're on the phone with friends. The instant your study symbol is associated with something *other* than studying, it begins to lose its effectiveness as a study aid.

Fighting Tiredness and Boredom

You've chosen the best study spot, and no one could fault you on its setup. So why are you still using pencils to prop up your eyelids? Here's what to do if your energy has taken a brief vacation:

- **Take a nap.** What a concept! When you're too tired to study, take a short nap to revive yourself. Maximize that nap's effect by keeping it short—20 minutes is ideal, 40 minutes absolute maximum. After that, you go into another phase of sleep and you may wake even more tired than before.

- **Have a drink.** A little caffeine won't harm you—a cup of coffee or tea, a glass of soda. Just be careful not to mainline it—caffeine's "wake-up" properties seem to reverse when you reach a certain level, making you far more tired than you were!

- **Turn down the heat.** You needn't build an igloo out back, but too warm a room will inevitably leave you dreaming of sugarplums…while your paper remains unwritten on your desk.

- **Shake a leg.** Go for a walk, high step around the kitchen, do a few jumping jacks—even mild physical exertion will give you an immediate lift.

- **Change your study schedule.** Presuming you have some choice here, find a way to study when you are normally more awake and/or most efficient.

Studying with Small Kids

Since so many more of you are going to school while raising a family, I want to give you some ideas that will help you cope with the Charge of the Preschool Light Brigade:

- **Plan activities to keep the kids occupied.** The busier you are in school and/or at work, the more time your kids will want to spend with you when you *are* home. If you schedule *some* time with them, it may be easier for them to play alone the rest of the time, especially if you've created projects *they* can work on while you're working on your homework.

- **Make the kids part of your study routine.** Kids love routine, so why not include them in yours? If 4 p.m. to 6 p.m. is always "Mommy's Study Time," they will soon get used to it, especially if you make spending other time with them a priority and give them something to do during those hours. Explaining the importance of what you're doing—in a way that includes some ultimate benefit for *them*—will also motivate them to be part of your "study team."

- **Use the television as a babysitter.** While many of you will have a problem with this—it's one that I and my daughter dealt with weekly, if not daily—it may be the lesser of two evils. And you can certainly rent (or DVR or TiVo) enough quality shows so you don't have to worry about the little darlings watching street gangs bash skulls in (or bashing skulls themselves on some video game system).

- **Plan your study accordingly.** All of these suggestions will not keep your kids from interrupting every now and then. While you can minimize such intrusions, it's virtually impossible to eliminate them entirely. So don't try—plan your schedule *assuming* them. For one, that means taking more frequent breaks to spend five minutes with your kids. They'll be more likely to give you the 15 or 20 minutes *you* need if they get periodic attention themselves.

- **Find help.** Spouses can occasionally take the kids out for dinner and a movie. (And trust me, the kids will encourage you to study more if you institute this practice!) Relatives can babysit (at their homes) on a rotating basis. Playmates can be invited over (allowing you to send your darling to their house the next day). You may be able to trade babysitting with other parents at school. And professional day care may be available at your child's school or in someone's home for a couple of hours a day.

Find Out Where You Shine

It is the rare individual who is superior, or even good, in *every* subject. If you are, count your blessings. Most of us are a little better in one subject or another. Some of us simply *like* one subject more than another—and don't think *that* doesn't change your attitude toward it. Others are naturally gifted in one area, average in others.

For example, skill with numbers and spatial relationships may come easily to you, but you may have absolutely no ear for music or languages. Or you may find learning a language to be a piece of cake, but not have the faintest clue why Pythagoras came up with his Theorem—or why you should care. Some students are good with their hands. Others (I'm in this group) may find making the simplest item torturous (and the results laughable).

The reasons for such unequal distribution of native-born talents rest somewhere in the area between karma and God, depending on your philosophy.

My advice is to be thankful for whatever native-born talents you possess and use the gift as a double-edged sword. Shift some study time from those tasks easily achieved to those that you find more difficult. The balance you will see in your development will be well worth the effort.

And if you've never really thought about the subjects you like and dislike, use the chart at the end of this chapter to identify them. You'll also be asked to identify those in which you perform well or poorly. (Your report card should confirm those!) Use this list to organize your own schedule to take advantage of your natural talents and give added time to the subject areas that need the most work.

And If You Have a Choice

All college students—and some high school students—are able to pick and choose courses according to their own schedules, likes, dislikes, goals, etc. The bliss of such freedom should be tempered with the commonsense approach you're trying to develop through reading this book. Here are a few hints to help you along:

- Whenever possible, consider each professor's reputation as you decide whether to select a particular course, especially if it is an overview or introductory course offered in two or three sessions. Word soon gets around as to which professors' lectures are stimulating and rewarding—an environment in which learning is a joy, even if it isn't a subject you like!

- If there's a course you think you'd like to take but suspect or know you can't fit it in this semester (or even this year), take the time *now* to check out course requirements, assignments, reading lists, etc., and *go to the first class*. This is generally an overview of the entire course and the time when most professors hand out syllabuses, longterm assignments, and suggested reading lists. You may not be sure you want to take the course before that class, but you'll certainly have a better idea afterwards.

- Attempt to select classes that balance your schedule on a weekly and even a daily basis, though this will not always be possible or advisable. (Don't change your major just to fit your schedule!) Try to leave an open hour or half-hour between classes— it's ideal for review, postclass note taking, quick trips to the library, etc.

- Try to alternate challenging classes with those that come more easily to you. Studying is a process of positive reinforcement. You'll need encouragement along the way.

- Avoid late evening or early morning classes, especially if such scheduling provides you with large gaps of "downtime." And if you're not a "morning person," don't even think of taking a class that meets daily at 8 a.m. I did it my freshman year of college and managed to get there, oh, at least three times.

- Set a personal study pace and follow it. Place yourself on a study diet, the key rule of which is: *Don't overeat*.

The landscape is littered with the shadows of unsuccessful students who have failed in their pursuits—*not* because they lacked the talent or motivation, but because they just overloaded on information and pressure.

You *can* be successful without killing yourself!

Evaluation of Subject Areas

List the subject areas/courses you like most:

_____

_____

_____

_____

_____

_____

List those you like least:

_____

_____

_____

_____

_____

_____

List the courses in which you get the best grades:

_____

_____

_____

_____

_____

_____

And those in which you get the worst grades:

_____

_____

_____

_____

_____

_____

CHAPTER 3

HOW TO READ
AND REMEMBER

Personally, I'll read anything handy, just to be able to read *something*. But the fact that I have always loved to read didn't make it any easier to face some of those deadly textbook reading assignments. As a student, you inevitably will be required, as I was, to spend hours poring through ponderous, fact-filled, convoluted reading assignments for subjects that are required, but not exactly scintillating.

You may love reading for pleasure but have trouble reading textbook assignments for certain subjects. You may get the reading done but forget what you've read nearly as quickly as you read it. Or you just may hate the thought of sitting still to read *anything*. Whatever kind of student you are—and whatever your level of reading skill—this chapter will help you surmount your reading challenge.

And that includes, for those of you long out of school, reading those nap-inducing business tomes, trade magazine articles, and other work-related stuff that's rarely reader-friendly.

You'll learn what you *should* read—and what you don't *have* to. You'll discover how to cut down on the time you spend reading, how to identify the main idea and the important details, and how to remember more of what you read.

Who knows? I might even convince you reading is fun!

Define Your Purpose for Reading

What is your purpose for reading? If the best answer you can come up with is, "Because my teacher said I had to," we need to uncover some better reasons. Reading a chapter just so you can say, "I finished my assignment" is relatively futile. You may as well put the book under a pillow and hope to absorb it by osmosis.

Unless you identify some purpose for reading, you will find yourself flipping the pages of your textbooks while retaining little more than the chapter titles.

According to reading experts, there are six fundamental purposes for reading:

1. To grasp a certain message.
2. To find important details.
3. To answer a specific question.
4. To evaluate what you are reading.
5. To apply what you are reading.
6. To be entertained.

Using the Clues in Your Textbooks

There are special sections found in nearly all textbooks and technical materials (in fact, in almost all books except novels) that contain a wealth of information and can help you glean more from your reading. Becoming familiar with this data will enrich your reading experience and often make it easier. Here's what to look for:

The first page after the title page is usually the *table of contents*—a chapter-by-chapter list of the book's contents. Some are surprisingly detailed, listing every major point or topic covered in each chapter.

The first prose section (after the title page, table of contents, and, perhaps, an acknowledgments page) is the *preface*, usually a description of the information you will find in the book. Authors may also use the preface to point out unique aspects of their books.

The *introduction* may be in place of or in addition to the preface and may be written by the author or some "name" the author has recruited to lend additional prestige to his or her work. Most introductions are an even more detailed overview of the book—chapter-by-chapter summaries are often included to give the reader a feel for the material to be covered.

Footnotes may be found throughout the text (a slightly elevated number following a sentence or quote, e.g., "jim dandy"[24]) and either explained at the bottom of the page on which they appear or in a special section at the back of the text. Footnotes may be used to cite sources of direct quotes or ideas and/or to further explain a point, or to add information outside of the text. You may make it a habit to ferret out sources cited in this way for further reading.

If a text tends to use an alarmingly large number of terms with which you may not be familiar, the considerate author will include a *glossary*—essentially an abridged dictionary that defines all such terms.

The *bibliography*, usually at the end of the book, may include the source material the author used to research the textbook, a list of "recommended reading," or both. It is usually organized alphabetically by subject, making it easy for you to find more information on a specific topic.

Appendices containing supplementary data or examples relating to subject matter covered in the text may also appear in the back of the book.

The last thing in a book is usually the *index*, an alphabetical listing that references, by page number, every mention of a particular name, subject, and topic in the text.

Making it a habit to utilize all of these tools in your textbooks can only make your studying easier.

Find Other Textbooks if Necessary

Few textbooks are written by what most of us would even remotely call professional writers. While the authors might well be experts, even legends, in their particular fields, writing in jargon-free, easy-to-grasp prose is probably not their strong suit. You will occasionally be assigned a textbook that is so obtuse you aren't sure whether to read it front to back, upside down, or inside out.

If you find a particular chapter, section, or entire textbook as tough to read as getting your baby brother to do you a favor, get to the library or a bookstore and find *another* book covering the *same* subject area that you *can* understand. You might even consider asking your teacher or professor for recommendations. She will probably make your job of finding a *readable* text a lot easier. You may even score some brownie points for your seeming initiative (as long as you don't wonder aloud what caused her to select that torturous text in the first place!).

"Ron," I hear you grumbling, "what happened to the 'study smarter, not harder' bit? This can't *possibly* be a timesaver. Heck, I'll bet the books don't even cover the subject in the same way, let alone follow the same sequence! I'll be stuck slogging through *two* books."

Possibly. But if you just don't get it, maybe it's because the *author* just doesn't know how to *explain* it. *Maybe it's not your fault!* Too many students have sweated, moaned, dropped classes, even changed majors because they thought they were dumb, when it's possible it's the darned textbook that's dense, not you. So instead of continuing to slog though the mire, find an expert who can actually write—they're out there—and learn what you need to. If the other text finally helps you understand the subject, you'll find the original textbook much easier to fathom...presuming you need it at all.

Use the Clues in Each Chapter

Begin with a very quick overview of the assignment, looking for questions that you'd like answered. Consider the following elements of your reading assignment *before* you begin your reading:

Chapter titles and boldfaced subheads announce the detail about the main topic. And, in some textbooks, paragraph headings or boldfaced "lead-ins" announce that the author is about to provide finer details.

So start each reading assignment by going through the chapter, beginning to end, *reading* only *the boldfaced heads and subheads.*

Look for end-of-chapter summaries. Knowing what the author is driving at will help you look for the important building blocks for his conclusions while you're reading.

Most textbooks, particularly those in the sciences, will have charts, graphs, numerical tables, maps, and other illustrations. Be sure to observe how they supplement the text and what points they emphasize, and make note of these.

In some textbooks, you'll discover that key terms and information are highlighted within the body text. To find the definitions of these terms may then be your purpose for reading.

Some textbook publishers use a format in which key points are emphasized by questions, either within the body of or at the end of the chapter. If you read these questions *before* reading the chapter, you'll have a better idea of what material you need to pay closer attention to.

If you begin your reading assignment by seeking out these heads, subheads, and other purpose-finding elements of the chapter, you'll have completed your prereading step. I advise that you *always* preread every assignment.

Three Ways to Read

Depending on what you're trying to accomplish in a particular reading assignment and the kind of book involved, there are three different ways to read. Knowing when to use each will make any assignment easier:

1. **Quick reference reading** focuses on seeking specific information that addresses a particular question or concern the reader might have.
2. **Critical reading** is used to discern ideas and concepts that require a thorough analysis.
3. **Aesthetic or pleasure reading** is for sheer entertainment or to appreciate an author's style and ability.

The Importance of Prereading

The best way to begin any reading assignment is to skim the pages to get an overall view of what information is included. Then read the text more carefully and highlight it and/or take notes in your notebook.

A brief digression: Most everyone I know confuses "skim" and "scan." Let me set the record straight. *Skim is to read quickly and superficially. Scan is to read carefully but for a specific item.* So when you skim a reading selection, you are reading it in its entirety, though you're only hitting the "highlights." When you scan a selection, you are reading it in detail but only until you find what you're looking for. Scanning is the *fastest* reading rate of all—although you are reading in detail, you are *not* seeking to comprehend or remember anything that you see until you find the bit of information you're looking for.

You probably are assigned a lot of reading that can be accomplished by skimming for facts. By establishing the questions you want answered *before* you begin to read, you can quickly browse through the material, extracting only the information you need.

Let's say you're reading a science book with the goal of identifying the function of a cell's nucleus. You can breeze through the section that gives the parts of the cell. You can skim the description of what cells do. You already know what you're looking for—and there it is in the section that talks about what each cell part does. Now you can start to *read*.

By identifying the questions you wanted to answer (*a.k.a.* your purpose) in advance, you would be able to skim the chapter and answer your questions in a lot less time than it would have taken to painstakingly read every word.

Skimming, or prereading, is a valuable step even if you aren't seeking specific facts. When skimming for a general overview, there's a very simple procedure to follow:

1. If there is a title or heading, *rephrase it as a question*. This will be your purpose for reading.

2. Examine all the *subheadings, illustrations, and graphics*, as these will help you identify the significant matter within the text.

3. Read thoroughly the *introductory paragraphs*, the summary, and any questions at the chapter's end.

4. Read the *first sentence* of every paragraph, which generally contains the main point of the paragraph.

5. *Evaluate* what you have gained from this process: Can you answer the questions at the end of the chapter? Could you intelligently participate in a class discussion of the material?

6. *Write* a brief summary that encapsulates what you have learned from your skimming.

7. Based on this evaluation, *decide* whether a more thorough reading is required.

As a general rule, if you are reading textbook material word for word, you probably are wasting quite a bit of your study time. Good readers are able to discern what they should read in this manner and what they can afford to skim. When trying to simply gather detail and facts, skimming a text is a simple and very important shortcut that can save you a lot of reading time. Even if a more in-depth reading is necessary, you will find that by having gone through this process, you will have developed the kind of skeletal framework that will make your further reading faster, easier, and more meaningful. And if all you need is "Just the facts, ma'am," your ability to scan a selection, chapter, or book will save you minutes, if not hours, every week.

Whether you're skimming or scanning, you will have equipped yourself with the ability to better digest whatever the author is trying to communicate.

Seek Word Clues, Too

While the heads, subheads, first sentences, and other author-provided hints we've talked about will help you get a quick read on what a chapter is about, some of the words in that chapter will help you concentrate on the important points and ignore the unimportant. Knowing when to speed up, slow down, ignore, or really concentrate will help you read both faster and more effectively.

When you see words such as "likewise," "in addition," "moreover," "furthermore," and the like, you should know that nothing new is being introduced. If you already know what's going on, speed up or skip what's coming entirely.

On the other hand, when you see words like "on the other hand," "nevertheless," "however," "rather," "but," and their ilk, slow down—you're getting information that adds a new perspective or contradicts what you've just read.

Lastly, watch out for "payoff" words such as "to summarize," "in conclusion," "therefore," "consequently," "thus"—especially if you only have time to "hit the high points" of a chapter or you're reviewing for a test. Here's where everything that went before is happily tied up in a nice bow and ribbon, a present that enables you to avoid having to unwrap the entire chapter.

Now Go Back for Detail

If a more thorough reading is required, turn back to the beginning. *Read one section (chapter, unit, whatever) at a time.*

As you read, make sure you know what's going on by asking yourself if the passage is written to address one of these five questions:

1. **Who?** The paragraph focuses on a particular person or group of people. The topic sentence tells you *who* this is.
2. **When?** The paragraph is primarily concerned with *time*. The topic sentence may even begin with the word "when."
3. **Where?** The paragraph is oriented around a particular place or location. The topic sentence states *where* you are reading about.

4. **Why?** A paragraph that states reasons for some belief or happening usually addresses this question. The topic sentence answers *why* something is true or *why* an event happened.

5. **How?** The paragraph identifies the way something works or the means by which something is done. The topic sentence explains the *how* of what is described.

Do not go on to the next chapter or section until you've completed the following exercise:

1. Write definitions of any key terms you feel are essential to understanding the topic.

2. Write questions and answers you feel clarify the topic.

3. Write any questions for which you *don't* have answers—then make sure you find them through rereading, further research, or asking another student or your teacher.

4. Even if you still have unanswered questions, move on to the next section and complete numbers one to three for that section. (And so on, until your reading assignment is complete.)

The Challenge of Technical Texts

What about the unique challenges posed by highly technical texts—physics, trigonometry, chemistry, calculus— you know, subjects that three-fourths of all students avoid like the plague? These subjects demand a logical, organized approach and a step-by-step reading method. And they require a detection of the text's *organizational devices*.

Developing the skill to identify the basic sequence of the text will enable you to follow the progression of thought, a progression that is vital to your comprehension and retention.

Why? In most technical writing, each concept is a like a building block of understanding—if you don't understand a particular section or concept, you won't be able to understand the *next* section, either.

Most technical books are saturated with ideas, terms, formulas, and theories. The chapters are dense with information, compressing a great wealth of ideas into a small space. They demand to be read very carefully.

In order to get as much as possible from such reading assignments, you can take advantage of some devices to make sense of the organization. Here are five basics to watch for:

1. Definitions and terms.
2. Examples.
3. Classifications and listings.
4. Use of contrast.
5. Cause-effect relationships.

In reading any specialized text, you must begin at the beginning— understanding the jargon particular to that discipline. Familiar, everyday words have very precise definitions in technical writing. Everyday words can have a variety of meanings, some of them even contradictory, depending on the context in which they're used.

In contrast, in the sciences, terminology has fixed and specific meanings. For example, the definition of elasticity (*the ability of a solid to regain its shape after a deforming force has been applied*) is the same in Los Angeles or Las Palmas. Such exact terminology enables scientists to communicate with the precision their discipline requires.

Definitions may vary in length. One term may require a one-sentence definition; others merit entire paragraphs. Some may even need a whole chapter to accurately communicate the definition.

Look for key words that indicate specific mathematical operations. You need to *add* when you see words such as "increased by," "combined," "together," "sum," or "total of"; *subtract* when you see "decreased by," "minus," "less," "difference"; *multiply* when you see "product," "increased," "by a factor of," and "times"; and *divide* when you see "per," "ratio," "quotient," or "percent."

Another communication tool is the example. Authors use examples to bridge abstract principles to concrete illustrations. These examples are essential to your ability to comprehend intricate and complicated theories.

Unlike other writing, technical writing places a very high premium on brevity. Economizing words is the key to covering a large volume of knowledge in a relatively small space. Few technical texts or articles include anecdotal matter or chatty stories on the author's experiences.

This fact challenges the reader to pay particular attention to the examples that are included. Why? Technical writing often is filled with new or foreign ideas—many of which are not readily digestible. They are difficult in part because they are abstract. Examples work to clarify these concepts, hopefully in terms that are more easily understood.

A third tool frequently utilized in texts is classification and listings. Classifying is the process by which common subjects are categorized under a general heading. Especially in technical writing, authors use classification to categorize extensive lists of detail.

A fourth tool used in communicating difficult information is that of comparing and contrasting. Texts use this tool to bring complicated material into focus by offering a similar or opposing picture. Through comparison, a text relates a concept to one that has been previously defined—or to one a reader may readily understand. Through con-trast, the text concentrates on the differences and distinctions between two ideas. By focusing on distinguishing features, these ideas become clearer as one idea is held up against another.

A final tool that texts employ to communicate is the cause-effect relationship. This device is best defined in the context of science, where it is the fundamental quest of most scientific research. Science begins with the observation of the effect—what is happening? *It is snowing*. The next step is to conduct research into the cause: *Why is it snowing?* Detailing this cause-effect relationship is often the essence of scientific and technical writing.

Cause-effect relationships may be written in many ways. The effect may be stated first, followed by the cause. An effect may be the result of several connected causes— a causal chain. And a cause may have numerous effects.

In your reading, it is vital that you recognize this relationship and its significance.

Read with a Plan

More than any other type of writing, highly specialized technical writing must be read with a plan. You can't approach your reading assignment merely with the goal of completing it. Such mindless reading will leave you confused and frustrated, drowning in an ocean of theories, concepts, terms, and examples.

Your plan should incorporate the following guidelines:

1. Learn the terms that are essential to understanding the concepts presented. Knowing the precise definitions that the author uses will enable you to follow his chain of thought through the text.

2. Determine the structure or organization of the text. Most chapters have a definite pattern that forms the skeleton of the material. A book may begin with a statement of a theory, give examples, provide sample problems, then summarize. Often this pattern can be discerned through a preview of the table of contents or the titles and subtitles.

3. Skim the chapter to get a sense of the author's viewpoint. Ask questions to define your purpose in reading. Use any summaries or review questions to guide your reading.

4. Do a thorough analytical reading of the text. Do not proceed from one section to the next until you have a clear understanding of the section you are reading—the concepts generally build upon each other. To proceed to a new section without understanding the ones that precede it is, at best, futile.

5. Immediately upon concluding your thorough reading, review! Write a summary of the concepts and theories you need to remember. Answer any questions raised when you skimmed the text. Do the problems. If possible, apply the formulas.

Technical material is saturated with ideas. When reading it, you must be convinced of one fact: Every individual word counts! You will want to read such material with the utmost concentration—it is not meant to be sped through.

Good readers know that such material demands a slow read that concentrates on achieving the greatest level of retention.

- Every definition has to be digested.
- Every formula must be committed to memory.
- Every example needs to be considered.

To improve your reading of such technical material, you will want to hone the skill of identifying the devices an author uses to communicate. In so doing, you will be able to connect the chain of thought that occurs. When reading such texts—or attempting to work out technical problems—try the following "tricks":

- Whenever you can, "translate" numbers and formulae into words. To test your understanding, try to put your translation into *different* words.

- Even if you're not particularly visual, pictures can often help. You should try translating a particularly vexing math problem into a drawing or diagram.

- Before you even get down to solving a problem, is there any way for you to estimate the answer or, at least, to estimate the range within which the answer should fall (greater than 1, but less than 10)? This is the easy way to at least make sure you wind up in the right ballpark.

- Play around. There are often different paths to the same solution, or even equally valid solutions. If you find one, try to find others. This is a great way to increase your understanding of all the principles involved.

- When you are checking your calculations, try working *backwards*. I've found it an easier way to catch simple mathematical errors.

- Try to figure out what is being asked, what principles are involved, what information is important, and what is not.

- Teach someone else. Trying to explain mathematical concepts to someone else will quickly pinpoint what you really know or don't know. It's virtually impossible to get someone else— especially someone who is slower than you at all this stuff— to understand if you don't!

Reading Foreign Language Texts

Foreign language texts should be approached the same way, especially basic ones teaching vocabulary. If you haven't mastered the words you're supposed to in the first section, you'll have trouble reading the story at the end of section three, even if you've learned all the words in sections two and three. So take it one step at a time and make sure you have mastered one concept, vocabulary list, lesson, and so forth, before jumping ahead.

Aesthetic (Pleasure) Reading

*"To read a writer is for me not merely to get an idea of what he says,
but to go off with him, and travel in his company."*
—Andre Gide

Most fiction is an attempt to tell a story. There is a beginning, in which characters and setting are introduced. There is a conflict or struggle that advances the story to a climax—where the conflict is resolved. A final *denouement* or "winding up" concludes the story. Your literature class will address these parts using terms that are often more confusing than helpful. The following are brief definitions of some of the more important ones:

Plot. The order or sequence of the story—how it proceeds from opening through climax. Your ability to understand and appreciate literature depends upon how well you follow the plot—the *story*.

Characterization. The personalities or characters central to the story—the heroes, the heroines, the villains, and the supporting characters. You will want to identify the main characters of the story and their relationships to the struggle and to each other.

Theme. The controlling message or subject of the story; the moral or idea that the author is using the plot and characters to communicate.

Setting. The time and place in which the story occurs. This is especially important when reading a historical novel or one set in another culture.

Point of view. Who is telling the story? Is it one of the central characters giving you flashbacks? Or is it a third-person narrator offering commentary and observations on the characters, the setting, and the plot?

The first step in reading literature is to familiarize yourself with these concepts, then try to recognize them in each novel or short story you read. As you begin your reading, approach it first from an aesthetic standpoint: How does it make you feel? What do you think of the characters? Do you like them? Hate them? Relate to them?

Second, make sure you know what's going on—this involves the plot and the development of the characters. On a chapter-by-chapter basis, you may find it helpful to keep a sheet of paper on which you can write a sentence or two on the plot development and note any new characters introduced.

How Fast Can You Understand?

"When we read too fast or too slowly, we understand nothing."
—Blaise Pascal

Are you worried that you read too slowly? You probably shouldn't be—less rapid readers are not necessarily less able. What counts is what you comprehend and remember. And like anything else, practice will probably increase your speed levels. If you must have a ranking, read the 500-word selection below, adapted from *Exploring Feng Shui* by Shawne Mitchell (New Page Books, 2004) from start to finish, noting the elapsed time on your watch. Score yourself as follows:

45 seconds or less	very fast
46–60 seconds	fast
61–90 seconds	high average
91–119 seconds	average
120–150 seconds	slow
151 seconds or more	very slow

The guiding philosophy of feng shui is that everything in the universe, including every one of us, is made of the same basic energy. This universal energy, known as chi (pronounced chee), is alive and has intelligence. Because on this fundamental level everything is in relationship with everything else, whenever anything changes, everything else also changes as a result.

Chi constantly ebbs and flows around and through us in ever-shifting patterns and levels of intensity. Modern science authenticated what the ancient Chinese art of feng shui has recognized for more than 4,000 years through the discovery that all matter and non-matter are composed of subatomic particles of energy. Quantum physicists have since done experiments that show that these infinitesimally small bits of energy literally respond to thought, changing their behavior depending on where and how researchers focus their attention. This revelation affirms the power of feng shui.

Imagine that a bubble of energy surrounds your body and extends 10 feet in every direction. As you move through the world, people and objects unavoidably pass through this bubble. Where your energy bubble intersects with the bubbles of others, a sort of comingling process takes place in which your energy responds to theirs and their energy responds to yours. Intangible thoughts and feelings can be communicated through these fields from person to person and by entering different spaces.

If the man sitting next to you on the bus were angry, his energy would feel "angry." You could read his state of being through your energy field even though you never held a conversation. If you walked into a church or temple where people have been praying for centuries, you likewise might pick up the energy signature of "peace" and "devotion" embedded in its walls and altars. The presence of anger and devotion would ripple into and through your field. You might also become angry or peaceful just by being exposed and responding to the energy of these emotions and thoughts.

Perhaps your energy bubble extends farther than 10 feet. Perhaps it is unlimited in scope, because at the subatomic level your personal energy is merely a drop in an entire sea of universal chi. In that case, every aspect of the world at large would impact you to a measurable degree. Everyone and everything on the planet in this scenario can be seen as interrelated and interdependent.

Consider the potential that this vision holds: We are all connected, part of the oneness of the universe. It is a point of orientation on which mystics and scientists, faith and logic, can agree. Although feng shui is not actually considered a spiritual practice or religion, it is a subtle and intuitive art that may ultimately enhance your spiritual beliefs. Furthermore, it is clear that the principles of energy are operating in our lives whether or not we are consciously attuned to them. Through feng shui, we can purposefully regulate the flow of positive energy in our environment and as a result enhance our lives.

What is the basic philosophy of feng shui? What is chi? Can you explain the concept of an "energy bubble?" What is the practical application of feng shui?

A good reader should be reading fast or very fast and have gotten at least three of the four questions correct. (Look back at the selection to find the answers.)

What Decreases Speed/Comprehension

- Reading aloud or moving your lips when you read.
- Reading mechanically—using your finger to follow words, moving your head as you read.
- Applying the wrong *kind* of reading to the material.
- Lacking sufficient vocabulary.

To Increase Reading Speed

- Focus your attention and concentration.
- Eliminate outside distractions.
- Provide for an uncluttered, comfortable environment.

- Don't get hung up on single words or sentences, but *do* look up (in the dictionary) key words that you must understand in order to grasp an entire concept.

- Try to grasp overall concepts rather than attempting to understand every detail.

- If you find yourself moving your lips when you read (vocalization), practice reading with a pen or some other (nontoxic, nonsugary) object in your mouth. If it falls out while you're reading, you know you have to keep working!

- Work on building your vocabulary. You may be reading slowly (and/or having trouble understanding what you read) because your vocabulary is insufficient for your reading level.

- Read more…and more often. Reading is a habit that improves with practice.

- Avoid rereading words or phrases. According to one recent study, an average student reading at 250 words per minute rereads 20 times per page. The slowest readers reread the most.

To Increase Your Comprehension

- Try to make the act of learning sequential— comprehension is built by adding new knowledge to existing knowledge.

- Review and rethink at designated points in your reading. Test yourself to see if the importance of the material is getting through.

- If things don't add up, discard your conclusions. Go back, reread, and try to find an alternate conclusion.

- Summarize what you've read, rephrasing it in your notes in your own words.

Most importantly, read at the speed that's comfortable for you. Though I *can* read extremely fast, I *choose* to read novels much more slowly so I can appreciate the author's wordplay. Likewise, any material that I find particularly difficult to grasp slows me right down. I read newspapers, popular magazines, and the like very fast, seeking to grasp the information but not worrying about every detail.

Should you take some sort of speed reading course, especially if your current speed level is low?

Reading for speed has some merit—many people who are slow readers read as little as possible, simply because they find it so tedious and boring. But just reading faster is not the answer to becoming a good reader.

I can't see that such a course could particularly *hurt* you in any way. I can also, however, recommend that you simply keep practicing reading, which will increase your speed naturally.

Remembering What You Read

In a world where the ability to master and remember a growing explosion of data is critical for individual success, too little attention is paid to the dynamics of memory and systems for improving it. Developing your memory is probably the most effective way to increase your efficiency, in reading and virtually everything else.

There are some key factors that will help you remember more of what you read:

- **Understanding.** You will remember only what you understand. When you read something and grasp the message, you have begun the process of retention. The way to test this is to rephrase the message in your own words. Can you summarize the main idea? Unless you understand what is being said, you won't be able to decide whether to remember or discard it.

- **Desire.** You remember what you *choose* to remember. If you do not want to retain some piece of information or don't believe you *can*, then you *won't*! To remember the material, you must *want* to remember it and be convinced that you *will* remember it.

- **Overlearn.** To ensure that you retain material, you need to go beyond simply doing the assignment. To really remember what you learn, you should learn material thoroughly, or overlearn. This involves prereading the text, doing a critical read, and having some definite means of review that reinforces what you should have learned.

- **Systematize.** It's more difficult to remember random thoughts or numbers than those organized in some pattern. For example, which phone number is easier to remember: 538–6284 or 678–1234? Once you recognize the pattern in the second number, it takes much less effort to remember than the first. You should develop the ability to discern the structure that exists and recall it when you try to remember. Have a system to help you recall how information is organized and connected.

- **Association.** It's helpful to attach or associate what you are trying to recall to something you already have in your memory. Mentally link new material to existing knowledge so that you are giving this new thought some context in your mind.

Retention

Retention is the process by which we keep imprints of past experiences in our minds, the "storage depot." Subject to other actions of the mind, what is retained can be recalled when needed. Things are retained in the same order in which they are learned. So your studying should build one fact, one idea, and one concept upon another.

Broad concepts can be retained more easily than details. Master the generalities, and the details will fall into place.

If you think something is important, you will retain it more easily. So convincing yourself that what you are studying is something you *must* retain (and recall) *increases* your ability to add it to your long-term memory bank.

Retention is primarily a product of what you understand. It has little to do with how *fast* you read, how great an outline you can construct, or how many fluorescent colors you use to highlight your textbooks. Reading a text, grasping the message, and remembering it are the fundamentals that make for high-level retention. Reading at a 1,000-words-per-minute clip does not necessarily mean that you understand what you've read or will remember any of it.

As you work toward improving your reading, realize that speed is secondary to comprehension. If you can read an assignment faster than anyone in class, but can't give a one-paragraph synopsis of what you just read, you've wasted your time. If you really get the author's message— even if it takes you an hour or two longer than some of your friends—spending the time you need to actually understand what you are reading will pay huge dividends in class and later in life.

Recall

This is the process by which we are able to bring forth those things that we have retained. Recall is subject to strengthening through the process of repetition. *Recall is least effective immediately after a first reading*, which is why periodic review is so important. The dynamics of our ability to recall are affected by several factors:

- We most easily recall those things that are of interest to us.
- Be selective in determining how much you need to recall. All information is not of equal importance— focus your attention on being able to recall the most *important* pieces of information.

- Allow yourself to react to what you're studying. Associating new information with what you already know will make it easier to recall.

- Repeat, either aloud or in your mind, what you want to remember. Find new ways of saying those things that you want to recall.

- Try to recall broad concepts rather than isolated facts.

- Use the new data you have managed to recall in a meaningful way—it will help you recall it the next time.

Recognition

This is the ability to see new material, recognize it for what it is, and understand what it means. Familiarity is the key aspect of recognition—you will feel that you have "met" this information before, associate it with other data or circumstances, then recall the framework in which it logically fits.

If you've ever envied a friend's seemingly wondrous ability to recall facts, dates, and telephone numbers virtually at will, take solace that, in most cases, *this skill is a result of study and practice*, not something he was born with.

There are certain fundamental memory systems that, when mastered, can significantly expand your capability. It is beyond the scope of this book to teach you all of these techniques; but if you feel you need help, I recommend *Improve Your Memory,* another book in my *How to Study Program.* You'll probably find a number of helpful titles at your library as well.

Take Notes

Do you own the book you're reading? Do you not care about preserving it for posterity? Then use its margins for notes. Go beyond mere highlighting to assign some ranking to the facts conveyed by the text.

I used to use a little shorthand method to help me remember written materials. I'd draw vertical lines close to the text to assign levels of importance. One vertical line meant that the material should be reviewed; two indicated that the facts were very important; asterisks would signify "learn or fail" material. I'd insert question marks for material that I wanted one of my more intelligent friends or a teacher to explain to me further. I'd use circles to indicate the information I was dead sure would show up on the next test.

Interestingly, I found that the very act of assigning relative weights of importance to the text and keeping a lookout for test material helped me remember because it heightened my attention.

Become an Active Reader

I urge you to quiz yourself on written material to ascertain how well you retain it. If this doesn't work, try asking the questions *before* you read the material.

For instance, even though I have been an avid reader throughout much of my academic life, I had some trouble with the reading comprehension sections of standardized tests the first couple of times I attempted them. Why? I think I had a tendency to rush through these sections.

Then someone suggested to me that I read the questions *before* I read the passage. Presto! Great scores in reading comprehension (765 points on my verbal SAT for all of you doubters!).

While you won't always have such a ready-made list of questions, there are other sources—the summaries at the beginnings of chapters or the synopses in tables of contents. Pay attention to these.

This technique will train your mind to hone in on those important details when they arise in the story. It would also be a good idea to ask yourself these questions immediately after you finish the chapter. It will help you decide whether you "got" the important points of the chapter and help you retain the information longer.

Understand, Don't Memorize

Approach any text with the intent of *understanding* it rather than memorizing it. Understanding is a key part of memorization. Don't stop the flow of information during your reading (other than to underline and take notes). Go back and memorize later.

Organize the Material

Our minds crave order. Optical illusions work because the mind is bent on imposing order on every piece of information coming in from the senses. As you read, think of ways to organize the material to help your mind absorb it.

I always liked diagrams with single words and short phrases connected with arrows to show cause-and-effect relationships. Or I would use a special mark (a triangle) to highlight in texts the *reasons* things occurred.

Develop Good Reading Habits

It's difficult for anyone to remember what he read at 3 a.m. or while waiting to go on the biggest date of his life. Set aside quiet time when you're at your best. Are you a morning person? Then wake up early to do your reading. Do you get going at 6 p.m.? Then get your reading done before heading out to dinner.

Don't forget to use your dictionary to look up terms you don't understand.

Why We Forget

As you think about the elements of developing good memory, you can use them to address why you *forget*. The root of poor memory is usually found in one of these areas:

- We fail to make the material meaningful.
- We did not learn prerequisite material.
- We fail to grasp what is to be remembered.
- We do not have the desire to remember.
- We allow apathy or boredom to dictate how we learn.
- We have no set habit for learning.
- We are disorganized and inefficient in our use of study time.
- We do not use the knowledge we have gained.

All of us are inundated with information every day, bombarded with facts, concepts, and opinions. We are capable of absorbing some information simply because the media drench us with it. In order to retain most information, we have to make a concerted effort to do so. We must make this same effort with the material we read.

In Case You Forgot

Each time you attempt to read something that you must recall, use this six-step process to ensure you'll remember:

1. **Evaluate the material and define your purpose** for reading. Identify your interest level and get a sense of how difficult the material is.
2. **Choose appropriate reading techniques** for the purpose of your reading.
3. **Identify the important facts.** Remember what you need to. Identify associations that connect the details you must recall.
4. **Take notes.** Use your own words to write a synopsis of the main ideas. Use an outline, diagram, or concept tree to show relationships and patterns. Your notes provide an important backup to your memory. Writing down key points will further reinforce your ability to remember.

5. **Review.** Quiz yourself on those things you must remember. Develop some system by which you review notes at least three times before you are required to recall. The first review should be shortly after you've read the material, the second a few days later, and the final one just before you are expected to recall. This process will help you avoid cram sessions.

6. **Implement.** Find opportunities to *use* the knowledge you have gained. Study groups and class discussions are invaluable opportunities to implement what you've learned.

Build Your Own Library

> "The reading of all good books is like conversation
> with the finest men of past centuries."
> —Rene Descartes

If you are ever to become an active, avid reader, access to books will do much to cultivate the habit. I suggest you "build" your own library. Your selections can and should reflect your own tastes and interests, but try to make them wide and varied. Include some of the classics, contemporary fiction, poetry, and biography.

Save your high school and college texts—you'll be amazed at how some of the material retains its relevance. And try to read a good newspaper every day to keep current and informed.

Your local librarian can refer you to any number of lists of the "great books," most of which are available in inexpensive paperback editions. You may want to put some of these on your to-buy list, especially if you're planning a summer reading program. In *Improve Your Reading*, I have included my own lists of "great" authors and books. You may want to consult them as well.

Reading the classics—ancient and contemporary—will probably make you a better reader; it will certainly make you more well-read. That is the extra bonus for establishing such a reading program—an appreciation of certain authors, certain books, and certain cultural events is what separates the cultured from the merely educated and the undereducated.

Read On

Insofar as one can in a single chapter, I've tried to sum up the essentials of reading. It is not a finite science, but rather a skill and appreciation that one can develop over time. Good grade school training is essential. And for those of you who have been able to identify problem areas, there are always remedial classes.

CHAPTER 4

HOW TO ORGANIZE YOUR TIME

"Those who make the worst use of their time
are the first to complain of its brevity."
—Jean de la Bruyere

We all have problems with time. We can't control it—
we can't slow it down or speed it up. We can't save it
up—all we can do is decide how we're going to spend it.
We invariably need more of it...and don't know where to find it. *Then*
we wonder where the heck it all went.

I'm sure many of you reading this are struggling with sometimes
overwhelming responsibilities and commitments. Some of you may
be so burned out that you've just given up. Those of you who aren't
probably figure it's your fault—if you just worked *harder*, spent *more*
time on your papers and assignments, wired yourself online 24/7—
then everything would work out just fine.

So you resign yourselves to caffeine-fueled all-nighters, cramming for tests, and forgetting about time-consuming activities like eating and sleeping. Trying to do everything—even when there's too much to do—without acquiring the skills to *control* your time, is an approach that will surely lead to frustration and failure.

Whether you're a book author typing as fast as you can to meet a publisher's deadline; a student juggling five classes and a part-time job; or a parent working, attending classes, and raising a family; a simple, easy-to-follow time-management system is crucial to your success. And despite your natural inclination to proclaim that you just don't have the *time* to spend scheduling, listing, and recording, it's actually the best way to give yourself *more* time.

Why Do All This?

An organizational or time-management system that fits your needs can help you get more work done in less time. Whether your priority is more free time, improved grades, a less frantic life—or all of the above—learning how to organize your life and your studies can help you reach your objective, because an effective time-management system:

1. **Helps you put first things first.** Have you ever spent an evening doing a time-consuming assignment for an *easy* class, only to find that you hadn't spent enough time studying for a crucial test in a more difficult one?

2. **Helps you learn how long everything really takes.** One of the important components of this system is estimating how long each task will take you and tracking how long you actually spend doing it. Once you've inculcated this concept into your life, you'll finally discover where all that time you've been "losing" has been going.

3. **Reduces your tendency to procrastinate.** Once you have a realistic idea of the specific things you must accomplish and know that you have allocated sufficient time to do so, you're less likely to get frustrated and put them off.

4. **Helps you avoid time traps.** Time traps are the fires you have to put out before you can turn to tasks like studying. Time management is like a fire-*prevention* approach rather than a fire-*fighting* one: It allows you to go about your work systematically instead of moving from crisis to crisis or whim to whim.

5. **Helps you anticipate opportunities.** In addition to helping you balance study time with other time demands, effective time management can help make the time you *do* spend studying more productive.

6. **Gives you freedom and control.** Contrary to many students' fears, time management is *liberating*, not restrictive. A certain control over *part* of your day allows you to be flexible with the *rest* of your day.

7. **Helps you avoid time conflicts.** Simply having all of your activities, assignments, appointments, errands, and reminders written down in *one* place helps ensure that two or three things don't get scheduled at once. If time conflicts do arise, you will notice them well in advance and be able to rearrange things accordingly.

8. **Helps you avoid feeling guilty.** It is much easier to forget about studying if you've already allotted the time for it. Without a plan to finish the work you are doing, you may feel like it's "hanging over your head"—even when you're not working on it.

9. **Helps you evaluate your progress.** If you know you have to read an average of 75 pages a week to keep up in your business management class, and you've only read *60* pages this week, you don't need a calculator to figure out that you are slightly behind. And it's easy enough to schedule a little more time to read next week so you can catch up.

10. **Helps you see the big picture.** Effective time management provides you with a bird's-eye view of the semester. Instead of being caught off guard when the busy times come, you will be able to plan ahead—*weeks* ahead—when you have big tests or assignments due in more than one class.

11. **Helps you see the bigger picture.** Planning ahead and plotting your course early allows you to see how classes fit with your overall school career.

12. **Helps you learn how to study smarter, not harder.** It may well be possible that you will be *so* organized, *so* prioritized, *so in control of your time*, that you can spend *less* time studying, get *better* grades, and have *more* time for other things—extracurricular activities, hobbies, whatever.

Time management is *not* magic, though it can *appear* magical.

There May Not Be Enough Time for Everything

When I asked one busy student if she wished she had more time, she joked, "I'm *glad* there are only 24 hours in a day. Any more and I wouldn't have an excuse for not getting everything done!"

Let me give you the good news: There *is* a way that you can accomplish more in less time. And it *doesn't* take more effort. You *can* plan ahead and make conscious choices about how your time will be spent and how much time you will spend on each task. You *can* have more control over your time, rather than always running out of it.

Now the bad news: The first step to managing your time should be deciding just what is important…and what isn't. Difficult as it may be, sometimes it's necessary for us to recognize that we truly *can't* do it all, to slice from our busy schedules those activities that *aren't* that meaningful to us so we can devote more energy to those that *are*.

But There Is Enough Time to Plan

Even after paring down our commitments, most of us are still challenged to accomplish everything we need to. What with classes, study time, work obligations, extracurricular activities, and a social life, it's not easy fitting it all in.

The organizational plan that I outline in this book is designed particularly for students. Whether you're in high school, college, or graduate school, a "traditional" student or one who's chosen to return to school after being out in the "real world" for a while, you'll find that this is a manageable program that will work for you.

This program allows for flexibility. In fact, I encourage you to adapt any of my recommendations to your own unique needs. That means it will work for you whether you are living in a dorm, sharing accommodations with a roommate, or living with a spouse and children.

The purpose of this chapter is to help you make *choices* about what is important to you, set *goals* for yourself, *organize* and *schedule* your time, and develop the *motivation* and *self-discipline* to follow your schedule and reach those goals.

Wouldn't it be nice to actually have some extra *time*…instead of always wondering where it all went? To feel that you're exerting some control over your schedule, your schoolwork, your *life*…instead of caroming from appointment to appointment, class to class, assignment to assignment, like some crazed billiard ball?

It can happen.

Identify the Starting Line

You can't race off to your ultimate goal until you figure out where your starting line is. So the first step necessary to overhaul your current routine is to identify that routine in detail. There are two ways to go about this, and I suggest you do both.

The first is to use the chart on the next page to assess how much time you actually have available for studying. If it's clearly not enough, then you'd better reassess how much time you're spending in each of the other areas. You may have to cut your part-time work hours, quit a club, even change your schedule to reduce your commute. Of course, if you're spending two hours a day on "grooming" or six hours eating, the solution may be a little more obvious.

You should create a second chart yourself. Write down, in 15-minute increments, how you spend your time *right now*. While keeping track of your activities for a day or two might be sufficient for some of you, I recommend you chart them for an entire week, including the weekend.

This is especially important if, like many people, you have huge pockets of time that seemingly disappear, but in reality are devoted to things like "resting" after you wake up, putting on makeup or shaving, reading the paper, waiting for transportation, or driving to and from school or work. Could you use an extra hour or two a day, either for studying or for fun? Make better use of such "dead" time and you'll find all the time you need.

Where Does Your Time Go?

	Hrs./Day	Days/Wk	Hrs./Wk
Meals (including prep and cleanup)	_____	7	_____
Sleeping (including naps)	_____	7	_____
Grooming	_____	7	_____
Commuting	_____	5?	_____
Errands	_____	7	_____
Extracurricular activities	_____	_____	_____
Part- or full-time job	_____	_____	_____
In class	_____	_____	_____
Entertainment*	_____	_____	_____

*Hanging with friends, going out, watching TV, reading for pleasure, etc.

Fill in the first column, multiply by the second, then total the third column. There are 168 hours in a week (24 x 7). How many do you currently have left for studying? Note: Any answer that contains a minus is a *bad* sign.

Learn how to do multiple tasks at the same time: listen to a book on tape while you're working around the house; practice vocabulary or math drills while you're driving; or have your kids, parents, or roommates quiz you for an upcoming test while you are doing the dishes, vacuuming, or dusting. And always carry your calendar, notebook(s), pens, and a textbook with you—you can get a phenomenal amount of reading or studying done while in line at the bank, the library, the supermarket, or on a bus or train.

Strategy tip: Identify those items on your daily calendar, whatever their priority, that can be completed in 15 minutes or less. These are the ideal tasks to tackle during that "dead" time.

Collect What You Need

As you begin your planning session, make sure you have all the information and materials you need to make a quality plan. Gather your class syllabuses; work schedule; dates of important family events, vacations, trips, or other personal commitments (doctor appointments, birthday parties, etc.); and a calendar of any extracurricular events in which you plan to participate.

There are only two items you need to become the most organized person you know: a long-term planning calendar that can be tacked onto a wall and a daily calendar you can carry with you.

Keeping track of your day-to-day activities—classes, appointments, regular daily homework assignments, and daily or weekly quizzes— will be dealt with later in this chapter. For now, I want to talk about the projects—term papers, theses, studying for midterm and final exams, etc.—that require completion over a long period of time— weeks, maybe even months.

Your Long-Term Planning Calendar

It's not necessary for you to construct your own calendar, though it's certainly the least expensive alternative. There are ready-made wall and desk calendars available in a variety of formats for your convenience, including magnetic and erasable. Your local art supply, stationery, or bookstore will have a selection of them. I suggest at least a three-month calendar. You could certainly use a six-month or even a yearly calendar.

You will not be filling this calendar with a great deal of detail, so the spaces in which you will write do not have to be humongous. This calendar is the overview of your schedule, a kind of "life-at-a-glance" summary of those items and appointments *occurring more than one week in the future*. (If they are happening this week, they will be in your daily calendar, but I'm ahead of myself.)

So start by entering the date for every major test, when papers and projects are due, future appointments (yes, this isn't just for school-work), and anything else that you must remember. I have reproduced a single month from a typical calendar on page 94. Notice that there is little detail. It's a snapshot, remember?

Your Daily Calendar

This is the most essential tool you can utilize, and one you absolutely *must*. Find a format that works for you. I prefer one like that repro-duced on pages 96–97, with Monday, Tuesday, and Wednesday on a left-hand sheet and Thursday through Sunday on a right. Whether in a notebook or spiral-bound, this format gives you the entire week at a glance *and* more than enough room to write in great detail. I find that reason enough to avoid those appointment books that give you one day per page. You may get a lot more room to write, but you'll find yourself doing a lot of flipping around just to see what's happening tomorrow or the next day.

In the filled-in calendar on pages 96–97, our student—let's call her Lindsay—did a pretty good job. She didn't just jot down homework assignments. First, she prioritized them—those As, Bs, and Cs to the left of each entry.

Next, she estimated the amount of time each would take (in the "T" for "Time" column) and how long it actually took (in the "A" for "Actual" column). She used minutes, but you certainly can use fractions of an hour if you find it easier. Whatever total time you wind up allocating should approximate the time you actually have available. If you find yourself habitually spending more time on assignments than you have projected, consider adding a "safety margin" to your estimates. Then total all the estimates and make sure you haven't scheduled yourself till 4 a.m.!

Finally, Lindsay included more than just homework assignments—she jotted reminders to herself about grocery shopping, phone calls she had to make, band practice, and a host of other things.

There are also assigned projects that are not due this week—an English paper, an upcoming quiz in geometry, a bigger test in history. Lindsay scheduled time to choose a topic for her English paper, get the teacher's approval, and even begin preliminary research. She also planned time to study for both geometry and history.

The dates when future projects are due and future tests scheduled actually are recorded twice—once in her daily calendar, and again in her long-term calendar. But the steps necessary to write her paper and the time she needs to allocate for studying are only on her daily calendar. (This is not a hard-and-fast rule. You can certainly include steps necessary for future projects on your long-term planning calendar, too. I prefer not to muddle it up with too much detail.)

Unfortunately, Lindsay isn't doing the greatest job projecting how long her homework will actually take her. Geometry always takes her longer than she thinks it will, and her biology lab report clearly was more complicated than she expected. She scheduled five total hours for band rehearsal…but spent eight, which is probably why she failed to do any preliminary research for her English paper. And it's not clear whether she's scheduled "make-up time" during the next week.

If you set up and use your daily calendar this way, you will quickly discover it is your life. You will always carry it with you, and you will die a horrible death if you ever misplace it or, heaven forbid, lose it.

Leave your long-term planning calendar on your wall or desk at home, and carry your daily calendar with you— *everywhere*. Whenever new projects, appointments, meetings, etc., are scheduled, add them immediately to your daily calendar. Then transfer key dates to your long-term planning calendar.

Remember: If it's a simple task that will definitely be accomplished within a week or an event or appointment that is occurring that week—read pages 201–274, study for quiz, proofread a paper— it belongs in your daily calendar.

If, however, it's a task that is complicated—requiring further break-down into specific steps—and/or one that will require more than a week to complete—the final due date should be entered on your long-term calendar, *then* the individual steps should be added to your daily calendar.

Make Your First Appointment… with Yourself

For any time-management system to work, it has to be used continually. Before you go on, make an appointment with yourself for the end of the week—Sunday night is perfect—to sit down and plan for the following week. You don't have to spend a lot of time—half an hour is probably all it will take to review your commitments for the week and schedule the necessary study time.

Despite its brevity, this may just be the best time you spend all week, because you will reap the benefits of it throughout the week and beyond!

First, identify anything you need to do this week that is not yet written in on your daily calendar. Look at your long-term calendar to determine what tasks need to be completed this week for all of your major school projects. Add any additional tasks that must be done—from sending a birthday present to your sister to attending your monthly volunteer meeting to completing homework that may have just been assigned.

Remember to break any long-term or difficult projects into small, "bite-size" tasks that can be included on your schedule. As Henry Ford said, "Nothing is particularly hard if you divide it into small jobs." Hence, the assembly line.

Once you have created your list, you can move on to the next step—putting your tasks in order of importance.

Prioritize Your Tasks

When you sit down to study without a plan, you just dive into the first project that comes to mind. The problem with this approach has been discussed earlier: There is little guarantee that the first thing that comes to mind is the most important.

If you find yourself forgetting to transfer data back and forth from your long-term calendar to your daily calendar (or vice versa), or you simply need even more help keeping the most important tasks in mind, a Priority Task Sheet is another tool you can use. Its sole purpose is to help you arrange your tasks in order of importance (not to record them—that's the job of your calendar). That way, even if you find yourself without enough time for everything, you can at least finish the most important assignments. You can't effectively deal with today's priorities if you still have to contend with yesterday's…or last week's!

First, ask yourself this question: "If I only got a few things done this week, what would I want them to be?" Mark these high-priority tasks with an "H" or an "A." After you have identified the "urgent" items, consider those tasks that are least important—items that could wait until the following week to be done, if necessary. (This may include tasks you consider very important but that don't have to be completed this week.) These are low-priority items, at least for this week—mark them with an "L" or a "C."

All the other items fit somewhere between the critical tasks and the low-priority ones. Review the remaining items. If you're sure none of them are particularly low or high priority, mark them with an "M," for middle priority, or a "B."

Strategy tip: If you push aside the same low-priority item day after day, week after week, at some point you should just stop and decide whether it's something you need to do at all! This is a strategic way to make a task or problem "disappear." In the business world, some managers purposefully avoid confronting a number of problems, waiting to see if they will simply solve themselves through benign neglect. If it works in business, it can work in school. (But if you find yourself consistently moving "B" or even "A" priorities from day to day, reassess your system. Something's broken.)

A completed Priority Task Sheet is on page 95. A blank Priority Task Sheet you can photocopy is on page 98.

Have you been taking the time to estimate how long each task will take, and adjusting your projections when it's clear certain tasks invariably take longer than you think? Terrific! Here's a way to use such estimating as a great motivator: Instead of writing down how long a task will take, write down the time you intend to finish it. What's the difference? It has now become a goal. It may put just the slightest amount of pressure on you, making you try just a little harder to finish on time.

You can take this goal-setting technique further. Write down the times you expect to finish each page of a 10-page reading assignment, or each one of the 20 math problems you have to complete. Setting such small time goals is a great motivator and a fantastic way to maximize your concentration and minimize daydreaming.

And Keep in Mind...

Besides the importance of the task and the available time you have to complete it, other factors will determine how you fit everything you have to do into the time available. Some factors will be beyond your control—your work schedule, appointments with professors, counselors, or doctors. But there are plenty of factors you do control and should consider as you put together your calendar each week.

Schedule enough time for each task—time to "warm up" and get the task accomplished, but, particularly when working on long-term projects, not so much time that you "burn out." Every individual is different, but most students study best in blocks of 30–45 minutes, depending on the subject.

Don't overdo it. Plan your study time in blocks, breaking up work time with short leisure activities. (It's helpful to add these to your schedule as well.) For example, you've set aside three hours on Wednesday afternoon for that research assignment. Schedule a 15-minute walk to the ice cream shop somewhere in the middle of that study block. You'll find that these breaks help you think more clearly and creatively when you get back to studying.

Even if you tend to like longer blocks of study time, be careful about scheduling study "marathons"—a six- or eight-hour stretch rather than a series of one- or two-hour sessions. The longer the period you schedule, the more likely you'll have to fight the demons of procrastination and daydreaming. Convincing yourself that you are really studying your heart out, you'll also find it easier to justify time-wasting distractions, scheduling longer breaks, and, before long, quitting before you should.

Finally, remember Parkinson's Law: "Work expands so as to fill the time available for its completion." In other words, if you fail to schedule a one-hour block for a project that should take an hour, you will probably be surprised to find (eureka!) that it somehow takes two or three!

Strategy tip: Get into the habit of getting ready for the next day before you go to bed the night before. Believe me, it's an absolutely fantastic feeling to *start* the day completely organized…especially if you oversleep!

Using These Tools Effectively

There are thinkers, and there are doers.

And there are those who think a lot about doing.

Once you have discovered habits and patterns of study that work for you, continue to use and hone them. Be flexible enough to add techniques you learn from others and alter schedules that circumstances have made obsolete.

Plan according to *your* schedule, *your* goals, and *your* aptitudes, not some ephemeral "standard." Allocate the time you expect a project to take *you*, not the time it might take someone else or how long your teacher says it should take. Try to be realistic and honest with yourself when determining those things that require more effort or those that come easier to you.

Whenever possible, schedule pleasurable activities *after* study time, not before. They will then act as incentives, not distractions.

Monitor your progress at reasonable periods and make changes where necessary. This is *your* study regimen— you conceived it, you can change it. If you find that you are consistently allotting more time than necessary to a specific chore, change your future schedule accordingly.

As assignments are entered on your calendar, make sure you also enter items needed—texts; other books you have to buy, borrow, or get from the library; and materials such as drawing pads, magic markers, and graph paper.

You may decide that color-coding your calendar—say, red for assignments that must be accomplished that week, blue for steps in longer-term assignments, yellow for personal time and appointments, green for classes—makes it easier for you to tell at a glance what you need to do and when you need to do it.

Adapt these tools for your own use. Try anything you think may work—use it if it does, discard it if it doesn't.

Do your least favorite chores (study assignments, projects, whatever) first—you'll feel better having gotten them out of the way! And plan how to accomplish them as meticulously as possible. That will get rid of them even faster.

Accomplish one task before going on to the next one—don't skip around.

If you see that you are moving along faster than you anticipated on one task or project sequence, there is absolutely nothing wrong with continuing onto the next part of that assignment or the next project step.

If you're behind, don't panic. Just reorganize your schedule and find the time you need to make up.

Write things down. Not having to remember all these items will free up space in your brain for the things you need to concentrate on or *do* have to remember.

Learn to manage distractions. As a time management axiom puts it, "Don't respond to the urgent and forget the important." Some things you do can be picked up or dropped at any time. Beware of these time-consuming and complicated tasks that, once begun, demand to be completed. Interrupting at any point might mean starting all over again. What a waste of time *that* would be!

If you're writing and you have a brainstorm just as the phone rings (and you know it's from that person you've been waiting to hear from all week), take a minute to at least jot down your ideas before you stop.

Nothing can be as counterproductive as losing your concentration, especially at critical times. Learn to ward off those enemies that would alter your course, and you will find your journey much smoother.

One way to guard against these mental intrusions is to know your own study clock and plan accordingly. Each of us is predisposed to function most efficiently at specific times of day (or night). Find out what sort of study clock you are on and schedule your work during this period.

Beware of uninvited guests and all phone calls: Unless you are ready for a break, they'll only throw you off schedule. More subtle enemies include the sudden desire to sharpen every pencil in the house, an unheard-of urge to clean your room, an offer to do your sister's homework— anything to avoid your own work. If you find yourself doing anything *but* your work, either take a break then and there, or pull yourself together and get down to work. Self-discipline, too, is a learned habit that gets easier with practice.

The simple act of saying no (to others or to yourself) will help insulate you from these unnecessary (and postponable) interruptions. Remember, what you are seeking to achieve is not just time—but *quality* time. Put your "Do not disturb" sign up and stick to your guns, no matter what the temptation.

And if your schedule involves working with others, you need to take *their* sense of time into account—you may find you have to schedule "waiting time" for a chronically late friend…and always bring a book along.

A Special Note for Commuters

If you live at home (as opposed to being housed on campus), there are some special pressures with which you need to contend.

Your commute to school will probably be longer than if you could roll out of bed and walk to class. It will certainly require more wakefulness, even if you just have to stumble to a subway or bus (but especially if you have to drive!). It's especially important that you minimize travel time, planning enough to maximize your use of the campus facilities without scheduling a trip home in between.

While nobody likes walking to class in rain, sleet, or snow—except, perhaps, future postal employees—it is invariably easier to walk a few tree-lined blocks than drive a few miles in inclement weather. Take weather problems into account when scheduling your commute.

The very act of living at home—whether as a child or one "married with children"—brings with it responsibilities to others you could minimize living in a dorm. Be ready to allocate time to these responsibilities and include them in your schedule. They're as inevitable if you live at home as meatloaf on Tuesdays.

The Most Important 15 Minutes of Your Day

Set aside 15 minutes every day to go over your daily and weekly priorities. While many businesspeople like to make this the first 15 minutes of their day, I recommend making it the last 15 minutes of your day. Why? Three great reasons:

1. **Your ideas will be fresher.** It's easier to analyze at the end of the day what you've accomplished…and haven't.

2. **It's a great way to end the day.** Even if your "study day" ends at 11 p.m., you'll feel fully prepared for the next day and ready to relax, anxiety-free.

3. **You'll get off to a great start the next morning.** If you use the morning to plan, it's easy to turn a 15-minute planning session into an hour of aimless "thinking." While others are fumbling for a cup of coffee, you're off and running!

Long-term Calendar (Filled-in Sample)

MONTH: *January*

MON	TUE	WED	THU	FRI	SAT	SUN
1	2	3	4	5	6	7
	Gorbachev rough paper due			*French vocab quiz*	*mom visit*	↑
8	9	10	11	12	13	14
	English midterm	*Geometry midterm*	*History midterm*			
15	16	17	18	19	20	21
					Lacrosse tourney ↑	↑
22	23	24	25	26	27	28
		First 2 parts of French project due		*French vocab quiz*	*Lacrosse tourney* ↑	↑
29	30	31				

Priority Task Sheet (Filled-in Sample)

Priority Rating	Schedule	Priority Tasks This Week Week of 3/28 through 4/3
		Sociology paper
H		**Library search*
M		**Outline*
L		**Rough draft*
		Math assignments
H		**Chapter 4*
M		**Chapter 5*
M		**Study for test*

Daily Calendar (Filled-in Sample)

January

20		Monday	T	A	Notes
A	Geometry	probs 24–42 odd	40	60	pick up milk & eggs
A	History	Read Chap 3	30	40	Don't forget homework!
A	Biology	Finish lab report	60	25	
	Read CH. 8	30	25		
C	Choose English topic		20	15	
	Check with teacher		10	10	
A	Bring gym shorts tomorrow				
B	Call Cheryl right after sch.				
A	7PM Band rehearsal		120	180	

21		Tuesday	T	A	Notes
C	Health	Redo chart (due Fri)	30	20	
A	Geometry	24–42 Even	40	70	
B	Spanish	Essay rough draft	75	120	See Mr. Dawkins for
					Thursday Appt.
B	Band 6:30		120	150	

22		Wednesday	T	A	Notes
A	Spanish	Essay final draft	60	70	
	proof	30	30		
A	History	Chap 4	30	45	
B	Biology	Chap 9	30	45	
		probs p.112	50	30	

Daily Calendar (Filled-in Sample)

$$\boxed{\textit{January}}$$

23	Thursday	T	A	Notes
A	Finalize Health chart, proof	20	40	
B	research English paper	120	0	2:30 Mr. Dawkins
	(online)			@ Lib. office
				Bring gym shorts!
				Dr. Gevens 5PM
	Band 6:30	60	150	

24	Friday	T	A	Notes
B	Geometry probs 85-110	50	90	
				Jerry - Are u picking me
				up tonight?
				What time?
				Bring PJs
Call:	Rob 742-6891			Toothbrush
	Jack 742-2222			Makeup
	Ira 743-8181			CDs (see list)
	Cheryl 777-7777			

25	Saturday	T	A	Notes
A	Study for Geometry quiz	120	90	
B	Study for Hist. midterm	120	120	
	(Feb 3)			
A	Biology probs pp. 113-114	60	45	

26	Sunday	T	A	Notes
	ENJOY!			
				Call mom!
	Church 11AM			
	Brunch @ Amy's 2PM			

Priority Task Sheet

Priority Rating	Schedule	Priority Tasks This Week Week of _____ through _____

Daily Calendar

		T	A	Notes

		T	A	Notes

		T	A	Notes

CHAPTER 5

HOW TO EXCEL IN CLASS

Whatever your grade level, whatever your grades, whatever your major, whatever your ultimate career goal, we all have one thing in common: the classroom experience.

Most teachers utilize the classroom setting as an opportunity to embellish and interpret material covered in the text and other assigned readings. If you always complete your reading assignments before class, you'll be able to devote your classroom time to the new material the teacher will undoubtedly cover.

You've Got to Have Class

Exactly how you'll use the skills we'll cover in this chapter will be influenced by two factors: the type of classroom setup and the particular methods and styles employed by each of your teachers.

Each of the following general class formats will require you to make adjustments to accomplish your goals.

Lectures: Podium Pleasantries

Pure lectures are quite common from the college level up, but exist only rarely at the high school level. Lecture halls at larger colleges may fill up with hundreds of students for some of the more popular courses (or introductory classes, particularly in the sciences).

Primary emphases: listening; note taking.

Discussions: Time to Speak Your Mind

Also called *tutorials* and *seminars*, discussion groups are, again, common on the college level, often as adjuncts to courses boasting particularly large enrollments. A typical weekly schedule for such a course might consist of two lectures and one or more discussion groups. Often led by graduate teaching assistants, these discussion groups contain fewer students—usually no more than two dozen—and give you the chance to discuss points made in the lecture and material from assigned readings.

Such groups rarely follow a precise text or format and may wander wildly from topic to topic, once again pointing out the need for a general mastery of the course material, the "jumping off" point for discussion.

Primary emphases: asking/answering questions; analyzing concepts and ideas; taking part in discussion.

Combination: The Best (or Worst) of Both

Some postsecondary courses are, for want of a better term, combination classes—they combine the lecture and discussion formats (the typical kind of precollege class you're probably used to). The teacher prepares a lesson plan of material he or she wants to cover in a specific class. Through lecture, discussion, question and answer, audiovisual presentation, or a combination of one or more such devices, the material is covered.

Your preparation for this type of class will depend to a great extent on the approach of each individual instructor. Such classes also occur on the postsecondary level—college, graduate school, trade school— when class size is too small for a formal lecture approach.

Primary emphases: note taking; listening; participation; asking and answering questions.

Handson: Getting Your Hands Dirty

Classes such as science labs and various vocational education courses (industrial arts, graphics, and so forth) occur at all levels from high school up. They are concerned almost exclusively with *doing* something— completing a particular experiment, working on a project, whatever. The teacher may demonstrate certain things before letting the students work on their own, but the primary emphasis is on the student carrying out his or her own projects while in class.

On the college level, science labs are usually overseen by graduate assistants. Trade schools may use a combination of short lectures, demonstrations, and handson workshops; you can't become a good auto mechanic just by reading a book on cleaning a distributor.

Primary emphasis: development and application of particular manual and technical skills.

Exceptions to the Rule

Rarely can a single class be neatly pigeonholed into one of these formats, though virtually all will be primarily one or another. It would seem that size is a key factor in choosing a format, but you can't always assume, for example, that a large lecture course, filled with 200 or more students, will feature a professor standing behind a rostrum reading from his prepared text. Or that a small class of a dozen people will tend to be all discussion.

During my college years, I had a religion teacher who, though his class was one of the more popular on campus and regularly drew 300 or more students to each session, rarely lectured at all. I never knew *what* to expect when entering his classroom. One week it would be a series of musical improvisations from a local jazz band, with a variety of graduate assistants talking about out-of-body experiences. Another session would consist entirely of the professor arguing with a single student over one key topic…which had *nothing* to do with that week's (or any *other* week's) assignment.

In another class of merely 20 students, the professor teaching us physical chemistry would march in at the sound of the bell and, without acknowledging anyone's presence or saying a word, walk to the blackboard and start writing equations. He would wordlessly work his way across the massive board, until, some 20 or 30 minutes later, he ran off the right side. Slowly, he would walk back to the left side…and start writing all over again. He never asked questions. Never asked *for* questions. In fact, I'm not sure I remember him uttering *any*thing for three solid months!

Know Your Teacher

You must know and understand the kind of teacher you've got and his likes, dislikes, preferences, style, and what he expects you to get out of the class. Depending on your analysis of your teacher's habits, goals, and tendencies, preparation may vary quite a bit, whatever the topic or format of the class.

Take something as simple as asking questions during class, which I encourage you to do whenever you don't understand a key point. Some teachers are very confident fielding questions at any time during a lesson; others prefer questions to be held until the end of the day's lesson; still others discourage questions (or any interaction for that matter) entirely. Learn when and how each one of your teachers likes to field questions, then ask them accordingly.

No matter how ready a class is to enter into a free-wheeling discussion, some teachers fear losing control and veering away from their very specific lesson plan. Such teachers may well encourage discussion but always try to steer it into a predetermined path (their lesson plan). Other teachers thrive on chaos, in which case you can never be sure what's going to happen.

Approaching a class with the former type of teacher should lead you to participate as much as possible in the class discussion, but warn you to stay within whatever boundaries she has obviously set.

Getting ready for a class taught by the latter kind of teacher requires much more than just reading the text— there will be a lot of emphasis on your understanding key concepts, interpretation, analysis, and your ability to apply those lessons to cases never mentioned in your text at all!

Some teachers' lesson plans or lectures are, at worst, a review of what's in the text and, at best, a review plus some discussion of sticky points or areas he feels may give you problems. Others use the text or other assignments merely as a jumping-off point—their lectures or lesson plans might cover numerous points that aren't in your text at all. Preparing for the latter kind of class will require much more than rote memorization of facts and figures—you'll have to be ready to give examples, explain concepts in context, and more.

Most of your teachers and professors will probably have the same goals: to teach you how to think, learn important facts and principles of the specific subject they teach, and, perhaps, how to apply them in your own way.

In math or science classes, your ability to apply what you've learned to specific problems is paramount.

Other classes, such as English, will require you to analyze and interpret various works, but may emphasize the "correct" interpretation, too.

Whatever situation you find yourself in—and you may well have one or more of each of these "types"—you will need to adapt the skills we will cover in this chapter to each.

Adapt to Your Teacher's Style

All instructors (perhaps I should say all *effective* instructors) develop a plan of attack for each class. They decide what points they will make, how much time they will spend reviewing assignments and previous lessons, what texts they will refer to, what anecdotes they will use to provide comic relief or human interest, and how much time they'll allow for questions.

Building a note-taking strategy around each teacher's typical "plan of attack" for lectures is another key to academic success. Why do some students just seem to know what's important and what's not? How do they ferret out exactly the information that's "test-worthy" while not even glancing at the material that isn't?

What these students innately know is that items discussed during *any* lesson can be grouped into several categories:

- Information not contained in the class text(s) or other assigned reading.
- Explanations of obscure material covered in the text but with which students may have difficulty.
- Demonstrations or examples to further explain a concept, process, or subject.
- Background information to put course material in context.

As you listen to your teacher, try to figure out which category his remarks fall into. This will help you determine how detailed your notes on that segment of the lecture should be.

How to Prepare for Any Class

In general, here's how you should plan to prepare for any class before you walk through the door and take your seat.

Complete All Assignments

Regardless of a particular teacher's style or the classroom format she is using, virtually every course you take will have a formal text (or two or three or more) assigned to it. Though the way the text explains or covers particular topics may differ substantially from your teacher's approach to the same material, your text is still the basis of the course and a key ingredient in your studying. You *must* read it, plus any other assigned books, *before* you get to class.

You may sometimes feel you can get away without reading assigned books beforehand, especially in a lecture format where you know the chance of being called on is slim to none. But fear of being questioned on the material is certainly not the only reason I stress reading the material that's been assigned. You will be lost if the professor decides—for the first time ever!—to spend the entire period asking the students questions. I've had it happen. And it is not a pleasant experience for the unprepared.

You'll also find it harder to take clear and concise notes in class when you don't know what's in the text— in which case you'll be frantically taking notes on material you could have underlined in your books the night before. You'll also find it difficult to evaluate the relative importance of the teacher's remarks.

If you're heading for a discussion group, how can you participate without your reading as a basis? I think the lousiest feeling in the world is sitting in a classroom knowing that, sooner or later, you are going to be called on and you don't know the material.

Remember: Completing your reading assignment includes not just reading the *main* text but any *other* books or articles assigned, plus handouts that may have been previously passed out. It also means completing any nonreading assignments—turning in a lab report, preparing a list of topics, or being ready to present your oral report.

Needless to say, while doing your homework is important, *turning it in* is an essential second step! My daughter, Lindsay, refused to use any organizational system for a short time. As a result, in addition to a host of missed appointments and forgotten assignments, she would often forget to pack the homework she *did* do, or bring it to school but forget to turn it in.

One simple change I made in her routine has made a world of difference: She now has a bright red manila folder, marked "HOMEWORK," into which she puts every completed assignment the instant it's done. When she gets to class, she immediately pulls out her folder to see if she has something to turn in. (She's also given up on her "nonorganizational" system, but that's another story.)

Review Your Notes

Your teacher is probably going to start this lecture or discussion from the point she left off last time. And you probably won't remember where that point was unless you check your notes.

Have Questions Ready

This is your chance to find the answers to the questions that are still puzzling you. Review your questions before class. That way, you'll be able to check off the ones the teacher answers along the way and only need to ask those left unanswered.

Prepare Your Attitude

Don't discount the importance of the way you approach each class mentally. Getting the most out of school in general and any class in particular depends in good measure on how ready you are to really take part in the process. It is *not* sufficient, even if you're otherwise well-prepared, to just sit back and absorb the information. Learning requires your active participation every step of the way.

What to Do in Class

Keep in mind your own preferences and under what circumstances you do best—refer back to the first two chapters and review your skills lists. You'll need to concentrate most on those courses in which you do poorly.

Sit Near the Front

Minimize distractions by sitting as close to the instructor as you can.

The farther you sit from the teacher, the more difficult it is to listen. Sitting toward the back of the room means more heads bobbing around in front of you and more students staring out the window—encouraging you to do the same.

Sitting up front has several benefits. You will make a terrific first impression on the instructor—you might very well be the only student sitting in the front row. He'll see immediately that you have come to class to listen and learn, not just take up space.

You'll be able to hear the instructor's voice, and the instructor will be able to hear *you* when you ask and answer questions.

Finally, being able to see the teacher clearly will help ensure that your eyes don't wander around the room and out the windows, taking your brain with them.

So, if you have the option of picking your desk in class, sit right down in front.

Avoid Distracting Classmates

The gum cracker. The doodler. The practical joker. The whisperer. Even the perfume sprayer. Your classmates may be wonderful friends, entertaining lunch companions, and ultimate weekend party animals, but their quirks, idiosyncrasies, and personal hygiene habits can prove distracting when you sit next to them in class.

Knuckle cracking, giggling, whispering, and note passing are just some of the evils that can divert your attention in the middle of your math professor's discourse on quadratic equations. Avoid them.

Listen for Verbal Clues

Identifying noteworthy material means finding a way to separate the wheat—that which you *should* write down— from the chaff—that which you should *ignore*. How do you do that? By *listening* for verbal clues and *watching* for the nonverbal ones.

Many teachers will invariably signal important material in the way they present it—pausing (waiting for all the pens to rise), repeating the same point (perhaps even one already made and repeated in your textbook), slowing down their normally supersonic lecture speed, speaking more loudly (or more softly), or even simply stating, "I think the following is important."

There are also numerous words and phrases that should *signal* noteworthy material (and, at the same time, give you the clues you need to logically organize your notes): "First of all," "Most importantly," "Therefore," "As a result," "To summarize," "On the other hand," "On the contrary," "The following (number of) reasons (causes, effects, decisions, facts, etc.)."

Such words and phrases give you the clues to not just write down the material that follows, but also to put it in context—to make a list ("First," "The following reasons"); to establish a cause-and-effect relationship ("Therefore," "As a result"); to establish opposites or alternatives ("On the other hand," "On the contrary"); to signify a conclusion ("To summarize," "Therefore"); or to offer an explanation or definition.

Watch for Nonverbal Clues

Studies have shown that only a fraction of communication is conveyed in words alone. A great deal of the message we receive when someone is speaking to us comes from body language, facial expression, and tone of voice.

Most instructors will go off on tangents of varying relevance to the subject matter. Some of these will be important, but, at least during your first few lessons with that particular teacher, you won't know which.

Body language can be your clue. If the teacher begins looking out the window or his eyes glaze over, he's sending a clear signal: "This won't be on any test."

On the other hand, if he turns to write something down on the blackboard, makes eye contact with several students, and/or gestures dramatically, he's sending an equally obvious signal about the importance of the point he's making.

Teachers like to see students take notes. It shows you are interested in the topic and that you think enough of what is being said to write it down. (And, if you've ever stood at the front of the room, you can usually tell who's taking notes and who's writing a letter to a friend in Iowa.)

Ask Questions

No, don't raise your hand to ask or answer a question every 90 seconds. Being an active listener means asking *yourself* if you understand everything that has been discussed. If the answer is no, ask the instructor questions at an appropriate time or write down questions that you must have answered to fully understand the subject.

Challenge yourself to draw conclusions from the things the instructor is saying. Don't just sit there letting your hand take notes. Let your mind do something, too. Think about the subject matter—how it relates to what you've been assigned to read and other facts to which you've been exposed.

Learn How to be Selective

I'm sure you've observed in your classes that some people are constantly taking notes. Others end up with two lines on one page. Most of us fall in between.

The person who never stops taking notes is either writing a letter to that friend in Iowa or has absolutely no idea what *is* or is *not* important.

Taking concise, clear notes is first and foremost the practice of discrimination—developing your ability to separate the essential from the superfluous, to identify and retain key concepts, key facts, and key ideas, and ignore the rest. In turn, this requires the ability to listen to what your teacher is saying and copying down only what you need to understand the concept. For some, that could mean a single sentence. For others, a detailed example will be key.

Just remember: The quality of your notes usually has little to do with their *length*—three key lines that reveal the core concepts of a whole lecture are far more valuable than paragraphs of less important data.

So why do some people keep trying to take verbatim notes, convinced that the more pages they cover with scribbles the better students they're being? It's probably a sign of insecurity—they may not have read the material or have a clue about what's being discussed, but at least they'll have complete notes!

Even if you find yourself wandering helplessly in the lecturer's wake, so unsure of what she's saying that you can't begin to separate the important, noteworthy material from the nonessential verbiage, use the techniques discussed in this chapter to organize and condense your notes anyway.

If you really find yourself so lost that you are just wasting your time, consider adding a review session to your schedule (to read or reread the appropriate texts) and, if the lecture or class is available again at another time, attend again. Yes it *is*, strictly speaking, a waste of your precious study time, but *not* if it's the only way to learn and understand important material.

Take Notes on What You Don't Know

You *know* the capital of Germany. You *know* the chemical formula for salt. You *know* who's the current U.S. Secretary of State. So why waste time and space writing them down?

Frequently, your teachers will present material you already know in order to set the stage for further discussion or to introduce material that is more difficult. Don't be so conditioned to automatically copy down dates, vocabulary, terms, formulas, and names that you mindlessly take notes on information you already know. You'll just be wasting your time—both in class and later, when you review your overly detailed notes.

This is why some experts recommend that you bring your notes or outline of your textbook reading to class and *add your class notes to them*. I think it's an effective way to easily organize all your notes for that class.

Remember, taking effective notes requires five separate actions on your part:

1. *Listening* actively.
2. *Selecting* pertinent information.
3. *Condensing* it.
4. *Sorting/organizing* it.
5. *Interpreting* it (later).

Develop Your Shorthand Skills

Here are five ways to streamline your note taking:

1. Eliminate vowels. As a sign that was ubiquitous in the New York city subways used to proclaim, "If u cn rd ths, u cn gt a gd jb." (If you can read this, you can get a good job.) And, we might add, "u cn b a btr stdnt."
2. Use word beginnings ("rep" for representative, "Con" for Congressperson) and other easy-to-remember abbreviations.
3. Stop putting periods after all abbreviations (they add up!)
4. Use standard symbols in place of words. The following list, some of which you may recognize from math or logic courses, may help you:

≈	approximately
w/	with
w/o	without
wh/	which
→	resulting in
←	as a result of/consequence of
+	and or also
*	most importantly
cf	compare; in comparison; in relation to
ff	following
<	less than
>	more than
=	the same as
↑	increasing
↓	decreasing
esp	especially
Δ	change
⊂	it follows that
∴	therefore
b/c	because

5. Create your own symbols and abbreviations based on your needs and comfort level.

There are three specific symbols I think you'll want to create—they'll be needed again and again:

W   That's my symbol for "What?" as in "What the heck does that mean?"; "What did she say?"; or "What happened? I'm completely lost!" It denotes something that's been missed—leave space in your notes to fill in the missing part of the puzzle after class.

M   That's my symbol for "My thought." I want to separate my thoughts during a lecture from the professor's—put too many of your own ideas (without noting they *are* yours) and your notes begin to lose serious value!

T!   My symbol for "Test!" as in "I'm betting the farm this point is probably on the test, dummy, so don't forget to review it!!!"

Feel free to use your own code for these important instances; you certainly don't have to use mine.

You may also want to create specific symbols or abbreviations for each class. In chemistry, "TD" may stand for thermodynamics, "K" for the Kinetic Theory of Gases (but don't mix it up with the "K" for Kelvin). In English, "Sh" is the Bard, "LB" is Lord Byron, and "RP" are the Romantic Poets.

How do you keep everything straight? Create a list on the first page of each class's notebook or binder section for the abbreviations and symbols you intend to use regularly through the semester.

Just be careful—in your fervor to adopt my shorthand system, don't abbreviate so much that your notes are absolutely unintelligible to you almost as soon as you write them!

You may certainly choose to abbreviate less and write a little more. Whatever system you develop, just make sure it serves the right purpose: giving you the time to really *listen* to your instructors, rather than just furiously scribbling down what they say.

The Cornell System

Here's a well-known note-taking system many college students are taught. If it works for you, use it.

Start by drawing a vertical line two to three inches from the left side of your notebook paper. Take notes to the *right* of this line.

During the lecture: Take notes as you normally would—in paragraph form, outline, or using your own shorthand.

After the lecture: Reread your notes and reduce them to the key words that will help you recall the important points of the lecture. Write those key words and phrases in the *left*-hand column. As you get better at this, you will find that reviewing for a test will only require studying the left-hand column—short and concise—not the right.

Draw Your Way to Good Grades

The one problem with this whole note-taking system I've discussed is that many people find it more difficult to remember words rather than pictures, especially those who, on the "My Ideal Study Environment" chart in Chapter 2, claimed they received information best visually rather than orally.

Mapping is another way to take notes that stresses a more visual style—drawing or diagramming your notes rather than just writing them down.

Let me show you how to map the first few pages of this chapter as an example. Start with a clean sheet of paper and, boxed or circled in the center, write the main topic.

After deciding on the first major topic ("Utilizing skills depends on class format") and placing it on your map, add the detail:

Lectures (emphases: listening, note taking)

Discussions (emphases: asking/answering, analyzing, discussing)

Combination (emphases: as above)

Hands-on (emphasis: development/application of pertinent skills)

The second major topic ("Know your teacher") and those that follow take their place in the line or circle you've chosen in the direction you've chosen. I've completed a map containing four major topics on the following page.

Active Participation: A "Grade A" Approach

In many nonlecture classes, you will find that discussion, mostly in the form of questions and answers, is actively encouraged. This dialogue serves to both confirm your knowledge and comprehension of specific subject matter and to identify those areas in which you need work.

Whatever the format in which you find yourself, participate in any discussion to the best of your ability. Most teachers consider class participation a key ingredient in your semester grades. No matter how many papers and tests you ace, if you never open your mouth in class, you shouldn't be surprised if you get less than an A.

If you're having trouble following an argument or particular line of thought, ask for a review or for clarification. Based on the professor's preferences and the class format, ask the questions you feel need answers.

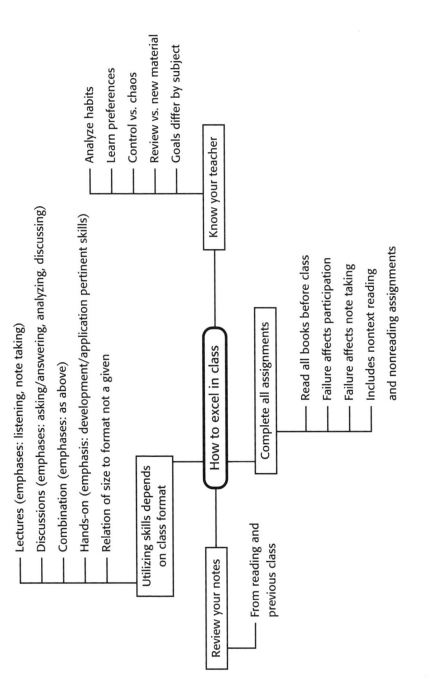

How to excel in class

Know your teacher
- Analyze habits
- Learn preferences
- Control vs. chaos
- Review vs. new material
- Goals differ by subject

- Lectures (emphases: listening, note taking)
- Discussions (emphases: asking/answering, analyzing, discussing)
- Combination (emphases: as above)
- Hands-on (emphasis: development/application pertinent skills)
- Relation of size to format not a given

Utilizing skills depends on class format

Complete all assignments
- Read all books before class
- Failure affects participation
- Failure affects note taking
- Includes nontext reading and nonreading assignments

Review your notes
- From reading and previous class

Be careful you don't innocently distract yourself from practicing your now-excellent note-taking skills by starting to analyze something you don't understand or, worse, creating mental arguments because you disagree with something your teacher or a classmate said. Taking the time to mentally frame an elaborate question is equally distracting. All three cause the same problem: You're not listening!

Finally, listen closely to the words of your classmates— you'll often find their comments, attitudes, and opinions as helpful and insightful as your instructor's.

What if you're shy or just get numb whenever you're called on? Ask a question rather than taking part in the discussion—it's easier and, over time, may help you break the ice and jump into the discussion. If you really can't open your mouth without running a fever, consider taking a public speaking course.

Most importantly, prepare and practice. Fear of standing in front of a class or even participating from the safety of your seat is, for many of you, really a symptom of lack of confidence.

And lack of confidence stems from lack of preparation. The more prepared you are—if you know the material backwards and forwards—the more likely you will be able to, even want to, raise your hand and "strut your stuff." Practicing with friends, parents, or relatives may also help.

If you are having trouble with oral reports, they are covered separately in Chapter 7. I think you'll find that the hints I've included there will eliminate a lot of the fear such talks seem to engender.

What to Do After Class

As soon as possible after your class, review your notes, fill in the "blanks," mark down questions you need to research in your text or ask during the next class, and remember to mark any new assignments on your weekly calendar.

I tend to discourage recopying your notes as a general practice, since I believe it's more important to work on taking good notes the first time around and not waste the time it takes to recopy. But if you tend to write fast and illegibly, it might also be a good time to rewrite your notes so they're readable, taking the opportunity to summarize as you go. The better your notes, the better your chance of capturing and recalling the pertinent material.

It is not easy for most high school students to do so, but in college, where you have a greater say in scheduling your classes, I recommend "one period on, one off"—an open period, even a half hour, after each class to review that class's notes and prepare for the next one.

If you find yourself unable to take full advantage of such in-between time, schedule as little time between classes as you can.

"Sleeping in" Isn't an Option

Even if you diligently apply all of the tips in this chapter, it will all be moot if you regularly miss class. So don't! It's especially important to attend all classes near semester's end. Teachers sometimes use the last week to review the entire semester's work (what a great way to minimize your own review time!), clarify specific topics they feel might still be fuzzy, and/or answer questions. Students invariably ask about the final exam during this period, and some teachers virtually outline what's going to be on the test!

If you must miss a class, find that verbatim note taker who hasn't followed my advice and borrow her notes. That way, you get to decide what's important enough to copy down. (Some professors might even lend you their notes. It's worth asking!)

Chapter 6

How to Conduct Your Research

Start any research project by working with the broadest outlines or topics (and the broadest resources) and slowly narrow your focus, getting more and more specific in topic and sources as you go along.

Encyclopedic entries are usually the most comprehensive and concise you will find. They cover so much territory and are so (relatively) up to date that they are an ideal "big picture" resource.

And don't forget to seek out a subject-specific encyclopedia. It seems there is such a tome on anything you can think of, to wit: *Encyclopedia of Christmas, Charlie Chan Film Encyclopedia, Encyclopedia of Paleontology, Encyclopedia of the Renaissance, Dictionary of Theology, A History of Women's Writing in France, Encyclopedia of Deserts, Encyclopedia of the Solar System, Encyclopedia of Human Nutrition, Encyclopedia of Smoking and Tobacco, Historical Encyclopedia of Nursing*, and the *Oxford Companion to Food*.

If you are writing a paper about a historical or contemporary figure, also consider skimming a biographical dictionary or, even better, one of the specific volumes in the *Who's Who* series, which ranges from *Who's Who in Art* and *Who's Who in American Jewry* to *Who's Who in Vietnam* and *Who's Who in Theatre*.

Needless to say, new CD-ROMs and reference websites appear almost hourly. These many current resources should make it increasingly easy to choose a good topic, establish a reasonable thesis, and gather enough information to construct an initial outline, without having to do any further research.

But completing an A+ paper will still require you to turn to other sources for more detailed information. You need to read books written by experts in the field you're researching, as well as magazine and newspaper articles about every aspect of your subject.

Why stop there? Pamphlets, anthologies, brochures, government documents, films, and videos are just some other possible sources of information for your paper.

Evaluating Resources

You may find so many potential resources that you won't have time to read them all. Concentrate on those that have been published most recently or written by the most respected sources. However, don't limit yourself *too* much—gather information from a wide range of sources. Otherwise, you may learn only one side of the story.

There are two types of resources: *primary* and *secondary*.

Primary resources are those written by people who *actually witnessed or participated in an event*. When you read a scientist's report about an experiment he has conducted, you are consulting a primary resource.

Secondary resources are those written by people *who were not actually present at an event*, but have studied the subject. When you read a book about the 1950s written by someone who was born in 1960, you are learning from a secondary resource.

Primary resources are likely to be more reliable sources of information. But depending upon your subject, there may not be any primary resources available to you.

Where to Look for Materials

How do you find out whether anyone has written a magazine or newspaper article about your topic? How do you know if there are any government documents or pamphlets that might be of help? How do you locate those written-by-the-experts reference books?

You look in your library's publication indexes, which list all of the articles, books, and other materials that have been published and/or are available in your library. Most are arranged alphabetically by subject:

1. **The card catalog.** This is a list of all the books in your library. (Although many libraries now store it on computer, it's still often called a card catalog because it used to be kept on index cards.) Books are indexed in three different ways: by subject, by author, and by title.

2. **Book catalogs.** The best-known are *Books in Print*, *Forthcoming Books*, and the *Cumulative Book Index*.

3. **Newspaper indexes.** Several large-city newspapers provide an indexed list of all articles they have published. Your library may even have past issues of one or more available on microfiche.

4. **Periodical indexes.** To find out if any magazine articles have been published on your subject, go to a periodical index. *The Readers' Guide to Periodical Literature*, which indexes articles published in the most popular American magazines, may be one with which you're already familiar.

5. **Vertical file.** Here's where you'll find pamphlets and brochures.

6. **Guide to U.S. Government Publications, American Statistical Index, and Congressional Information Service Index.** These are all useful for locating government publications.

7. **Computer databases.** Widely used indexes are available, covering American and world history, art, biology, philosophy, religion, psychology, engineering, and much more.

8. **The Internet.** Most magazines, newspapers, encyclopedias, government organizations, and so forth have websites that can be a starting point for your search. They often have links to other sites where you can find full-length articles and stories, biographic information, and the like.

Set aside solid blocks of time for your research. And remember: It's better to schedule a handful of extended trips to the library than 15 or 20 brief visits, better to do a solid few hours online than 10 minutes here and 15 minutes there.

How Libraries Are Organized

To provide organization and facilitate access, most small and academic libraries utilize the Dewey decimal classification system, which uses numbers from 000 through 999 to classify all material by subject matter. It begins by organizing all books into 10 major groupings.

Given the millions of books available in major libraries, just dividing them into these 10 groups would still make it quite difficult to find a specific title. So each of the 10 major groupings is further divided into 10, and each of these now 100 groups is assigned to more specific subjects within each large group. For example, within the philosophy classification (100), 150 is psychology and 170 is ethics. Within the history classification (900), 910 is travel and 930 is ancient history.

000–099	General
100–199	Philosophy
200–299	Religion
300–399	Social Sciences
400–499	Language
500–599	Natural Science and Mathematics
600–699	Technology
700–799	Fine Arts
800–899	Literature
900–999	General Geography and History

There is even further subdivision. Mathematics is given its own number in the 500 series—510. But specific subjects within mathematics are further classified: 511 is arithmetic, 512 is algebra, and so on.

Finally, to simplify your task even more, the last two digits in the Dewey code signify the type of book:

01   Philosophy of

02   Outlines of

03   Dictionary of

04   Essays about

05   Periodicals on

06   Society transactions and proceedings

07   Study or teaching of

08   Collections

09   History of

If your library doesn't use the Dewey system, it probably is organized according to the Library of Congress system, which uses letters instead of numbers to denote major categories:

A   General works (encyclopedias and other reference)

B   Philosophy, Psychology, and Religion

C   History: Auxiliary sciences (archeology, genealogy, etc.)

D   History General, non-American

E   American history (general)

F   American history (local)

G   Geography/Anthropology

H   Social sciences (sociology, business, economics)

J   Political sciences

K   Law

L   Education

M   Music

N   Fine arts (art and architecture)

P   Language/Literature

Q   Sciences

R   Medicine

S   Agriculture

T   Technology

U   Military science

V   Naval science

Z   Bibliography/Library science

Using Online Resources

There's so much material on the Internet, it's easy to be over-whelmed. While it can be extremely helpful to have access to some obscure websites that have just the material you need, especially when a book or two you want to take notes from has disappeared from the library, I am still convinced that most of you will waste too much time if the majority of your research is done online. I can attest from far too much personal experience that it is ridiculously easy to get sidetracked when doing research online. "Wow, I didn't know there were that many cool sites about bungee jumping. I'd better check them out…right now!"

Be careful about the following two things:

While much of the "basic" information on most research-oriented websites is not going to radically change from day to day, that is certainly not true of all sites. Just as the identical keyword search may yield radically different results if run on two separate days (or on two different search engines), you may find material you need deleted the next time you look for it. So if you find something really good, download it, save it to your hard drive, or print a hard copy.

Online bookstores (amazon.com, bn.com and, if you're Canadian, chapters.indigo.ca) will list many books even before they're published, and almost always before your local library has ordered, cataloged, and shelved them. Amazon's recently added feature of including searchable pages from many titles—from a table of contents and a short excerpt to 50 pages of text or more—should help you get a feel for whether the book or a portion of it is pertinent to your topic.

Amazon in particular offers a "People who bought this book also bought" feature, which is a good way to locate related resources (especially since none of the online bookstores make searches by subject easy or accurate).

An Approach to Online Research

I am indebted to Robin Rowland, author of *The Creative Guide to Research* (Career Press, 2001) for the following suggestions on how to maximize your time online:

- Long before a paper is due, choose four search engines—one a metasearch engine (which searches other search engines), the other three regular. Robin's recommendations: Copernic (meta), Google, Hotbot, AltaVista, Northern Light, Dogpile (meta).

- When beginning your research, use the meta engine first.
- Learn each engine's advanced features—you'll find things faster and easier.
- Print out the FAQ pages for each search engine and create your own manual.
- Choose three search engines with different strengths to maximize your search abilities.
- Consider using a specialized search engine, such as Beaucoup, if you are unable to find what you want or have found too much information.
- Learn Boolean searches.

There's no room in this book to list even a smattering of pertinent Internet sites. Wherever you go online, just remember:

- Some of the sites are informative and well-organized; some are quirky and skimpy.
- Some are well-researched and trustworthy; some are the rantings of a mad person. Just because something is on your computer screen doesn't mean it's true.
- Some provide unbiased information with no ulterior motive; some slant their information to sell you on their cause. Some are offering information just to entice you to buy something.
- Some are easy to use; some require you to search through listings to find what you need.
- Some supply information; some link you to other sites; some are simply listings of sites.
- Some may be gone when you look for them again.
- Some are free; some cost a bit…some cost a lot. Be sure to check out the cost before using a site where you have to pay.

Despite the immensity and importance of the Internet's resources, brick-and-mortar libraries are certainly not dinosaurs. Just because you can visit nearly any library in the world without leaving your computer screen is no reason to avoid becoming intimately familiar with your local or school library. You will find that doing *some* things online is not always as interesting, efficient, or fun as doing them "in person."

Chapter 7

How to Write Terrific Papers

Reading this chapter will not make you such a good writer that you can quit school and start visiting bookstores to preen in front of the window displays featuring your latest bestseller.

But there is absolutely no reason to fear a written paper or oral report, once you know the simple steps to take and rules to follow to complete it satisfactorily. Once you realize that 90 percent of preparing a paper has *nothing* to do with writing...or even being *able* to write. And once you're confident that preparing papers by following my suggestions will probably get you a grade or two higher than you've gotten before...even if you think you are the world's poorest excuse for a writer.

Doing a research paper requires a lot of work. But the payoff is great, too. You will learn, for example:

- How to track down information about *any* subject.
- How to sort through that information and come to a conclusion about your subject.
- How to prepare an organized, indepth report.
- How to communicate your ideas clearly and effectively.

Your teacher really didn't ask you to write a research paper just to make your life miserable. Of all the things you'll learn in school, the skills you acquire as you produce your research paper will be among the most valuable.

Five Fundamental Rules

Let's start with the fundamental rules that need to be emblazoned on your mind:

1. *Always* follow your teacher's directions to the letter.
2. *Always* hand in your paper on time.
3. *Always* hand in a clean and clear copy of your paper.
4. *Always* keep at least one copy of every paper you write.
5. *Never* allow a single spelling or grammatical error in any paper you write.

How Long Should It Be?

Your teacher's directions may include:

A general subject area from which topics should be chosen— "some aspect of Herbert Hoover's presidency," "a Civil War battle," "one of Newton's Laws," or "a short story by a 20th-century Russian writer."

- Specific requirements regarding format.
- Suggested length.
- Preferred methods for including footnotes and documenting works consulted (or cited).
- Other specific instructions.

Whatever his or her directions, *follow them to the letter*. Some high school teachers may forgive you your trespasses, but I have known college professors who simply refused to accept a paper that was not prepared as they instructed—and gave the poor student an F for it (without even *reading* it).

At some point, you'll undoubtedly run into a teacher or professor who gives few or no instructions at all. You ask, "How long should the paper be?" She says, "As long as it takes." Use your common sense. If you're in middle or high school, I doubt she is seeking a 50-page thesis. Likewise, if you're in college, it's unlikely your professor thinks a three-page paper is "As long as it takes." Use previous assignments as a guide.

If you are unsure of a specific requirement or if the suggested area of topics is unclear, it is *your* responsibility to talk to your teacher and clarify whatever points are confusing you.

It is not a bad idea to choose two or three topics you'd like to write about and seek preliminary approval, especially if the assignment seems particularly vague.

So Then My Dog Chewed the Paper . . .

There is certainly no reason, short of catastrophic illness or life-threatening emergency, for you to *ever* be late with an assignment. Again, some teachers will refuse to accept a paper that is late. At best, they will mark you down for your lateness, perhaps turning an A into a B...or worse. In the case of extenuating circumstances (e.g., extended illness, death in the family, and so on), let your teacher know immediately and arrange for an extension.

What's That Jelly Stain Worth?

Teachers have to read a lot of papers and shouldn't be faulted if, after hundreds of pages, they come upon your wrinkled, coffee-stained, pencil-written report and get a bit discouraged. Nor should you be surprised if you get a lower grade than the content might merit *just because the presentation was so poor*.

Granted, the content is what the teacher is looking for, and he *should* be grading you on *what* you write. But presentation *is* important. Teachers are only human (really!), and you can't fault them for trying to teach you to take pride in your work. So follow these suggestions:

- Never handwrite your paper.
- If you're using a computer, check the toner cartridge of your printer to ensure your printed pages are crisp and clear.
- Unless otherwise instructed, always double-space your paper. Leave adequate margins all around.
- Use a simple typeface that is clear and easy to read; avoid those that are too big—stretching a 5-page paper to 10— or too small and hard to read.
- Never use a fancy italic, gothic, modern, or other ornate or hard-to-read typeface for the entire paper.

Use Your Old Papers as Maps

There should be a number of helpful messages on your returned papers, which is why it's so important to retain them. What did your teacher have to say? Are her comments applicable to the paper you're writing now—poor grammar, lack of organization, lack of research, bad transitions between paragraphs, misspellings? The more such comments—and, one would expect, the lower the grade—the more extensive the "map" your teacher has given you for your next paper, showing you right where to "locate" your A+.

If you got a low grade on a previous paper but there weren't any comments, ask the teacher why you got such a poor grade. You may get the comments you need to make the next paper better *and* show the teacher you actually care, which could also help your grade the next time around.

Many employers merrily use resumes and cover letters with grammatical and/or spelling errors for wastebasket hoops practice. Don't expect your teachers to be any more forgiving—there are definitely a few out there who will award an F without even noticing that the rest of the paper is great. Guess it's just too bad you misspelled "Constantinople" or left a participle twisting slowly in the wind.

The Fry Paper-Writing System

The more complex a task or the longer you need to complete it, the more important your organization becomes. By breaking down any paper-writing project into a series of manageable steps, you'll start to feel less chaotic, hectic, and afraid right away.

Here are the steps that, with some minor variations along the way, are common to virtually any written report or paper:

1. Research potential topics.
2. Finalize topic.
3. Carry out initial research.
4. Prepare general outline.
5. Do detailed research.

6. Prepare detailed outline (from note cards).

7. Write first draft.

8. Do additional research (if necessary).

9. Write second draft.

10. Prepare final bibliography.

11. Spellcheck and proofread entire paper.

12. Have someone *else* proofread.

13. Produce final draft.

14. Proofread one last time.

15. Turn it in and collect your A+.

Create a Work Schedule

Doing all these tasks efficiently and effectively requires careful timing and planning. This may not be the only assignment—or even the only paper—you have to finish in a short amount of time.

So get out your calendar and mark the date your paper is due. How many weeks till then? Four? Six? Ten? Plan to spend from one-half to three-quarters of your time on research, the rest on writing.

Block out set periods of time during each week to work on your paper. Try to schedule large chunks of time—at least two or three hours, if possible—rather than many short periods. Otherwise, you'll spend too much time trying to remember where you left off and repeat steps unnecessarily.

As you plan your work schedule, set deadlines for completing the general steps of your paper-writing process. For example:

Week 1:   Decide on the topic and "angle" of your paper; make a list of reference materials.

Weeks 2–4:   Read reference materials; take notes.

Week 5:   Do detailed outline; write first draft.

Weeks 6–7:   Edit paper; prepare bibliography.

Week 8:   Proofread paper; print final copy.

Of course, I can't tell you exactly how much time to set aside for each step, because I don't know any of the specifics about your paper—how long it's supposed to be, how complex the topic—or how fast you work. I *can* tell you that you should plan on consulting and/or taking notes from at least six different sources. (Your teacher or subject may demand *more*; I doubt you'll need fewer.) And plan on writing two or three drafts of your paper before you consider it final.

Refer to your work schedule often, and adjust your pace if you find yourself lagging.

The more time you have to complete a project, the easier it is to procrastinate about dealing with it, even to putting off identifying the steps and working them into your regular schedule. If you find yourself leaving such long-term projects to the last week, schedule the projects furthest away—the term paper due in three months, the oral exam 10 weeks from now—*first*. Then, trick yourself—schedule the completion date at least seven days prior to the actual due date, giving yourself a one-week cushion for life's inevitable surprises. (Just try to forget you've used this trick. Otherwise, you'll be like the perennial latecomer who sets his watch 15 minutes fast in an effort to finally get somewhere on time. Except that he always reminds himself to add 15 minutes to the time on his wrist, defeating the whole purpose.)

Steps 1 & 2: Consider and Choose Topic Options

In some cases, your teacher will assign your topic. In others, she will assign a general area of study, but you will have the freedom to pick a specific topic.

There are some pitfalls you must avoid. Let's say you need to write a 15-page paper for your history class and decide your topic will be "The Presidency of Franklin Delano Roosevelt."

Can you really cover a topic that broad—*four* terms— in 15 pages? No, you can't. You could write volumes on the subject (people have) and still have plenty left to say!

Instead, you need to focus on a particular, limited aspect of such a broad subject or attack it from a specific angle. How about "Why FDR Tried to Pack the Supreme Court"? That would work for a middle school or high school paper.

Remember, your job is to prepare an *in-depth* report about your subject. Be sure you can do that in the number of pages your teacher has requested.

Choose a subject that's too *limited*, and you might run out of things to say on the second page of your paper. You might be able to write a couple of pages on "How FDR Contracted Polio," but you won't fill 10 or 15 pages…even with *really* wide margins.

If you can't find a single *book* on your supposed topic, rethink it! While there's nothing wrong with choosing a topic that can be researched via magazine articles, the newspaper, the Internet, and the like, why make your research so difficult if you don't have to?

Pick a topic that's too obscure, and you may find that little or no information has been written about it. In that case, you will have to conduct your own experiments, interview your own research subjects, and come up with your own original data. I'm guessing that you have neither the time, desire, nor experience to take such a start-from-scratch approach.

Don't bite off more than you can chew, but make sure there's *something* to gnaw on! And make sure that there are enough *different* sources of material—different authors, different books, different points of view—so you can get a well-rounded view of your subject (and not be forced, for lack of other material, to find ways to make somebody else's points sound like your own).

Taking all of the above into consideration, do a little brainstorming now about possible topics for your paper. Don't stop with the first idea—come up with several different possibilities. Put this book down until you have a list of three or four potential topics.

How about trying to get papers for two or more classes *out of the same research*? You may not be able to simply produce one paper for two classes, but with a little extra research—*not* what you would need to do for an entirely different paper—you may well utilize a good portion of the first paper as the basis for a second. What a great way to maximize your library time!

If you are having trouble choosing a topic for your next paper, here are two books that will help:

> *10,000 Ideas for Term Papers, Projects, Reports and Speeches: Intriguing, Original Research Topics for Every Student's Need*, 5th Edition, by Kathryn Lamm (Arco, 1998).

> *1001 Ideas for English Papers: Term Papers, Projects, Reports, and Speeches* by Walter James Miller (Hungry Minds, Inc., 1994).

Step 3: Begin Initial Library Research

Got your list? Then get thee to a library. You need to do a little advance research. Scan your library's card-catalog index and the *Readers' Guide to Periodical Literature* or other publication indexes. See how many books and articles have been written about each topic on your "possibilities" list. Next, read a short background article or encyclopedia entry about each topic.

Alternatively, spend a little time online. Are there specific websites devoted to your topic? Lucky you! Or does a keyword search result in 10,424 matches, none of which have a *thing* to do with your topic?

With any luck at all, you should be left with at least one topic that looks like a good research subject. If two or more topics passed your preliminary research test, pick the one that interests you most. You're going to spend a lot of time learning about your subject. There's no rule that says you can't enjoy it!

Develop a Temporary Thesis

Once you have chosen the topic for your paper, you must develop a temporary thesis. (The word "thesis" is a relative of "hypothesis" and means about the same thing—the central argument you will attempt to prove or disprove in your paper. A thesis is not the same thing as a *topic*. Your topic is what you study; your thesis is the conclusion you draw from that study.)

A "thesis statement" sums up the main point of your paper. It's generally just a sentence or two.

Note that I said *temporary* thesis. It may not wind up being your final thesis. Because you haven't completed all your research yet, you can only come up with a "best guess" thesis at this point.

If a temporary thesis doesn't spring easily to mind— and it probably won't—sit back and do some more brainstorming. Ask yourself questions like:

- What's special or unusual about _____? (Fill in the blank with your topic.)
- How is _____ related to events in the past?
- What impact has _____ made on society?
- What do I want the world to know about _____?
- What questions do I have about _____?

You may discover during this preliminary research phase that your temporary thesis just won't fly. You may have to revise it, perhaps even settling on a thesis that's the exact opposite of your original! In fact, you may have to revise your thesis several times during the course of your research.

Step 4: Create a Temporary Outline

Once you have developed your temporary thesis, think about how you might approach the subject in your paper. Jot down the various issues you plan to investigate. Then come up with a brief, temporary outline of your paper, showing the order in which you might discuss those issues.

Step 5: Do Detailed Research

We've already reviewed library and online resources and how to take advantage of them. Now, let's talk about exactly how you'll keep track of all the resources and information you'll gather for your paper.

There are two steps involved. First, you'll create bibliography cards for each source you want to review. Then, you'll transfer all the information from your bibliography cards to a single list—your working bibliography.

This two-step method has been around since someone wrote the first research paper, and with good reason: It works! It helps you conduct your research in an organized, efficient manner *and* makes preparing your final bibliography easier.

To create your working bibliography, you'll need a supply of 3 × 5 index cards. You'll also use index cards when you take notes for your paper, so buy a big batch now. About 300 cards ought to suffice. While you're at it, pick up one of those little file boxes designed to hold the cards. Put your name, address, and phone number on the file. If you lose it, some kind stranger can (and hopefully will) return it.

Start a systematic search for any materials that might have information related to your paper. When you find a book, article, or other resource that looks promising, take out a blank note card. On the front of the card, write down the following information:

In the upper right-hand corner of the card: Write the library call number (Dewey decimal number or Library of Congress number), if there is one, or the complete URL. Add any other detail that will help you locate the material on the library shelves (e.g., Science Reading Room, Reference Room, Microfiche Periodicals Room). And make sure to write down the *complete* website address.

On the main part of the card: Write the author's name, if given— last name first, followed by first name, then middle name or initial. Then the title of the article, if applicable, in quotation marks. Then the name of the book, magazine, newspaper, website, or other publication— underlined. (If you've already written the complete URL in the right-hand corner of the card, you do not need to duplicate it.)

Add any details you will need if you have to find the book or article again, such as:

- Date of publication.
- Edition—e.g., "third (1990) edition" for a book; "morning edition" for a newspaper.
- Volume and/or issue number.
- Page numbers on which the article or information appears.

Again, it is essential to write down the exact and complete URL, not just that of the main website. Navigating a complex site to find that short quote you wrote down can waste a lot of time.

In the upper left-hand corner of the card: Number it. The first card you write will be #1, the second, #2, and so on. If you happen to mess up and skip a number somewhere along the line, don't worry. It's only important that you assign a different number to each card.

Do this for *each* potential source of information you find, *and put only one resource on each card*. And leave some room on the card—you'll be adding more information later.

Citing Online Information

Because students are increasingly using online sources, the Modern Language Association (MLA) and American Psychological Association (APA), which publish style guides for research papers, have integrated electronic citations into their latest editions.

The MLA Handbook for Writers of Research Papers by Joseph Gibaldi (for high school and undergraduate college students) is now available in a seventh edition (2009). *The MLA Style Manual and Guide to Scholarly Publishing*, 3rd Ed. (2008), also by Gibaldi, is for graduate students, scholars, and professional writers. *The Publication Manual of the APA*, 6th Ed. (2009) is not available for free online, but detailed examples can be found at a number of addresses.

Another good source to consult is *Research and Documentation in the Electronic Age* by Diana Hacker (Bedford/St. Martins, 2004), which details citations using both styles.

Here is a sample online citation:

> Furfaro, John P. and Maury B. Josephson. "Reasonable Accommodation to Disability Act." *New York Law Journal*.
>
> http://homepages.go.com/~atlanticcity/040299 c4.htm (2 April 1999)

Sample Bibliography Card for a Book

1	315.6

Main Reading Room

Spechler, Jay W.

Reasonable Accommodation: Profitable Compliance
with the Americans with Disabilities Act
(see esp. pp. 54–61)

Computer Card Catalog
College Library

Sample Bibliography Card for a Magazine Article

2   www.timeinc.com/pub/2003/index.html

Smolowe, Jill

"Noble Aims, Mixed Results"
Time
(July 31, 2003; pp. 54–55)

Sample Bibliography Card for a Newspaper Article

3   www.nytimes/index/404/5.html

Wade, Betsy

"Disabled Access to Inns at Issue"
The New York Times
(April 14, 2004, section 5, page 4)

Getting Ready to Take Notes

Your bibliography cards serve as the map for your information treasure hunt. Get out a stack of five or six cards and locate the materials listed on those cards. Set up camp at a secluded desk or table and get to work.

When you write your paper, you'll get all the information you need from your notes, rather than from the original sources. Therefore, it's vital that you take careful and complete notes. What sort of information should you put in your notes? Anything related to your subject, and especially to your thesis. This includes:

1. General background information (names, dates, historical data).
2. Research statistics.
3. Quotes by experts.
4. Definitions of technical terms.

You may be used to keeping your notes in a three-ring binder or notepad. I'm going to show you a better way— recording all of your notes on index cards.

Let's say that you have found a reference book that contains some information about your subject. Before you begin taking notes, get out the bibliography card for that book.

Check that all of the information on your card is correct. Is the title exactly as printed on the book? Is the author's name spelled correctly? Add any other information you'll need to include in your final bibliography. (For more information on exactly what you need to include, be sure to refer to the newest edition of *Improve Your Writing*. It includes details on bibliographic and source note formats.)

Note-taking Guidelines

Once your bibliography card is finished, set it aside. Get out some blank index cards and start taking notes from your reference source. Follow these guidelines:

- **Write one thought, idea, quote, or fact on each card…and *only* one.** If you encounter a very long quote or string of data, you can write on both the front and back of a card, if necessary. *But never carry over a note to a second card*.

  What if you *can't* fit the piece of information on one card? Break it into two or more smaller pieces, then put each on a separate card.

- **Write in your own words.** Summarize key points about a paragraph or section or restate the material in your own words. Avoid copying things word for word.

- **Put quotation marks around any material copied verbatim.** It's okay to include in your paper a sentence or paragraph written by someone else to emphasize a particular point (providing you do so on a limited basis). But you must copy such statements *exactly as written* in the original—every word, every comma, every period. You also must *always* put such direct quotes within quotation marks in your paper and credit the author.

Add Detail to Your Note Cards

As you finish each note card, do the following:

- **In the upper left-hand corner of the card**, write down the resource number of the corresponding bibliography card (from its left-hand corner). This will remind you where you got the information.

- **Below the resource number**, write the page number(s) on which the information appeared.

- **Get out your preliminary outline.** Under which outline topic heading does the information on your card seem to fit? Under your "I" heading? Under "III"? Jot the appropriate Roman numeral in the upper right-hand corner of your note card. (You can use capital letters or even regular numbers if you prefer—just match whatever you used on your outline.)

  If you're not sure where the information fits into your outline, put an asterisk (*) instead of a topic letter. Later, when you do a more detailed outline, you can try to fit these "miscellaneous" note cards into specific areas.

- **Next to the topic letter**, jot down a one- or two-word "headline" that describes the information on the card.

- **When you have finished taking notes from a particular resource**, put a check mark on the bibliography card. This will let you know that you're done with that resource, at least for now.

Be sure that you transfer information accurately to your note cards. Double-check names, dates, and other statistics. As with your bibliography cards, it's not really important that you put each of these elements in the exact places I've outlined here. You just need to be consistent. Always put the page number in the same place, in the same manner. Ditto with the resource number, the topic heading, and the headline.

Add Your Personal Notes

Throughout your note-taking process, you may want to create some "personal" note cards—your own thoughts, ideas, or impressions about your subject or your thesis.

Write each thought on a separate note card, just as you did information taken from other resources. Assign your note card a topic heading and mini-headline, too. In the space where you would normally put the number of the resource, put your own initials or some other symbol. (I use "M" for "My Thought.") This will remind you that *you* were the source of the information or thought.

Step 6: Prepare a Detailed Outline

Your research is done.

Which means that at least *one-half* of your *paper*— perhaps as much as *three-quarters* of it—is done, even though you've yet to write one word of the first draft.

It's time to organize your data. You need to decide if your temporary thesis is still on target, determine how you will organize your paper, and create a detailed outline.

This is where the notecard system really pays off. Your note cards give you a great tool for organizing your paper. Get out all of your note cards, and then:

1. Group together all of the cards that share the same outline topic number or letter (in the right-hand corner of each card).

2. Put those different groups in order, according to your temporary outline.

3. Within each topic group, sort the cards further. Group the cards that share the same "headline" (the two-word title in the upper right corner).

4. Go through your miscellaneous and personal cards, the ones you marked with an asterisk or your own symbol. Can you fit any of them into your existing topic groups? If so, replace the asterisk with the topic number or letter. If not, put the card at the very back of your stack.

Your note cards now should be organized according to your preliminary outline. Take a few minutes to read through your note cards, beginning at the front of the stack and moving through to the back. *What you are reading is a rough sketch of your paper*—the information you collected in the order you (temporarily) plan to present it.

Does that order still make sense? Or would another arrangement work better? Here are some of the different organizational approaches you might consider for your paper:

1. **Chronological.** Discusses events in the order in which they happened (by time of occurrence).

2. **Spatial.** Presents information in geographical or physical order (from north to south, top to bottom, left to right, inside to outside, and so forth).

3. **Numerical/Alphabetical.** An obvious way to organize a paper on "The Ten Commandments" or "The Three Men I Admire Most," for example.

4. **Major division.** For topics that logically divide into obvious parts.

5. **How to**…grow an orchid, write a better paper, etc. Like this book, organizes material from "what to do first" to "what to do last."

6. **Problem/solution** (*a.k.a.* cause/effect). Presents a series of problems and possible solutions, why something happened, or predicts what *might* happen as a result of a particular cause.

7. **Effect/cause.** Discusses a condition, problem, or effect and works *backward* to what might have caused it.

8. **Compare/contrast.** Discusses similarities and differences between people, things, or events. May also be used when you want to discuss advantages and disadvantages of a method, experiment, treatment, approach, etc.

9. **Order of importance.** Discusses the most important aspects of an issue first and continues through to the least important, or vice versa. (A slight variation of this is organizing your paper from the *known* to the *unknown*.)

10. **Pro/con.** Arguments for and against a position, question, decision, approach, method, etc.

The first four sequences are considered "natural," in that the organization is virtually demanded by the subject. The other sequences are "logical," in that the order is chosen and imposed by *you*, the writer.

Note that in many cases the actual order you choose is also reversible—you can move forward or backward in time, consider cause and effect or effect and cause, etc. So you actually have a dozen and a half potential ways to organize your material!

Your subject and thesis may determine which organizational approach will work best. If you have a choice of more than one, use the one with which you're most comfortable or that you feel will be easiest for you to write. (Nobody says you *have* to choose the hardest way!) Keep in mind that you can use a *blend* of two approaches. For example, you might mention events in chronological order and then discuss the cause/effect of each.

If necessary, revise your general outline according to the organizational decision you have made. Next, go through each group of cards that share the same topic number or letter. Rearrange them so that they, too, follow the organizational pattern you chose.

After you sort all the cards that have been assigned a specific topic heading (I, II, III or A, B, C), review the cards that are marked with an asterisk or your personal symbol. Try to figure out where they fit in your stack of cards.

Don't include a card if the information it contains just doesn't seem to fit anywhere. It's possible that the data just isn't relevant to your revised thesis. Set it aside for now. You can try to include it again later.

And while you're setting aside inappropriate notes, don't forget to seek out "holes" in your paper—those areas that cry out for a more up-to-date fact, a good example, or a stronger transition. No one likes to discover the need to do a little more research, but if *you've* noticed a problem, I guarantee your teacher will, too. Don't let a "black hole" turn a potentially great paper into one that's merely okay just because you don't want to spend another hour online or in the library.

Now flip through your note cards from front to back. See that? You've created a detailed outline without even knowing it. The topic numbers or letters on your note cards match the main topics of your outline. And those headlines on your note cards are the subtopics for your outline.

Simply transfer your notecard headlines to paper. They appear on your outline in the same order as they appear in your stack of cards.

Step 7: Write the First Draft

You may not have realized it, but you've already *done* a lot of the hard work that goes into the writing stage. You have thought about how your paper will flow, you have organized your notes, and you have prepared a detailed outline. All that's left is to transfer your information and ideas from note cards to paper.

Good writing takes concentration and thought. And concentration and thought require quiet—and lots of it! You also need to have plenty of desk space, so you can spread out your note cards in front of you, your work area should be well-lit, and you should have a dictionary and thesaurus close at hand. If possible, "write" directly on to a computer, so you can add, delete, and rearrange your words at the touch of a button.

Remember: At this point, your goal is to produce a rough draft—with emphasis on the word "rough." Your first draft isn't supposed to be perfect. It's *supposed* to need revision. If you go into this thinking you're going to turn out a teacher-ready paper on your first try, you're doomed. That kind of performance pressure leads only to anxiety and frustration.

The essence of good writing has little to do with grammar, spelling, punctuation, and the like. The essence of good writing is good thinking.

Your thoughts, ideas, and logic are the foundation of your paper. And you need to build a house's foundation before you worry about hanging the front door. So, for now, just concentrate on getting your thoughts on paper. Don't worry about using exactly the "right" word. Don't worry about getting commas in all the right places. We'll take care of all that polishing later.

Your note cards helped you come up with a detailed outline. Now, they're going to help you plot out the actual paragraphs and sentences of your paper:

1. Your note cards should be arranged in the same order as your detailed outline. Take out all of the note cards labeled with the number or letter of the first topic on your outline.

2. Out of that stack, take out all the cards marked with the same "headline" as the first subheading in your outline.

3. Look at the information on those cards. Think about how the various pieces of information might fit together in a paragraph.

4. Rearrange those cards so they fall in the order you have determined is best for the paragraph.

5. Do this for each group of cards until you reach the end of the deck.

Each paragraph in your paper is like a mini-essay. It should have a topic sentence—a statement of the key point or fact you will discuss in the paragraph—and contain the evidence to support it. This evidence can come in different forms, such as quotes from experts, research statistics, examples from research or from your own experience, detailed descriptions, or other background information.

Stack up your paragraphs like bricks into your own "wall of evidence." Construct each paragraph carefully, and your readers will have no choice but to agree with your final conclusion.

If paragraphs are the bricks, transitions—a sentence or phrase that moves the reader from one thought to another—are the mortar holding them together. Smooth transitions help readers move effortlessly from one thought to another.

Now Put It All on Paper

Double- or triple-space your draft—that will make it easier to edit later. After you are finished with each note card, put a check mark at the bottom.

If you decide that you won't include information from a particular card, don't throw the card away—yet. Keep it in a separate stack. You may decide to fit in that piece of information in another part of your paper or change your mind after you read your rough draft and decide to include the information where you had originally planned.

You may, however, wind up with cards that just don't fit. If you're convinced they have no place in your paper, don't attempt to shoehorn them in anyway. Put them aside. As Johnny Cochran might proclaim, "If they blow the flow, those cards must go."

What If You Get Stuck?

Got writer's block already? Here are a few tricks to get you unstuck:

- Pretend you're writing to a good friend. Just tell him or her everything you've learned about your subject and why you believe your thesis is correct.

- Use everyday language. Too many people get so hung up on using fancy words and phrases that they forget that their goal is to *communicate*. Simpler is better.

- Just do it. Type *something…any*thing. Once you have written that first paragraph—even if it's a really *bad* first paragraph—your brain will start to generate spontaneous ideas.

- Don't edit yourself! As you write your rough draft, don't keep beating yourself up with negative thoughts, such as "This sounds really stupid" or "I'm a terrible writer. Why can't I express that better?" Remember: Your goal is a *rough* draft—it's supposed to stink a bit.

- Keep moving. If you get hung up in a particular section, don't sit there stewing over it for hours— or even for many minutes. Just write a quick note about what you plan to cover in that section, then go on to the next section. Force yourself to make it all the way through your paper, with as few stops as possible.

Freewriting and Brainstorming

Focused freewriting and brainstorming are two methods used by professional writers when the waters of creativity are dammed up somewhere in their brains. While similar, there are a couple of important differences between the two methods of getting started.

In both cases, set a brief time limit (perhaps 10 or 15 minutes), summarize your main topic in a phrase or sentence to get your thoughts moving, and do not edit or even review what you have written until the time is up.

Brainstorming is writing down everything you can think of *that relates to the topic*. It does not require that you work in any sequence or that your notes be logical or even reasonable. Asking yourself questions about the topic, no matter how strange, may help you generate new ideas.

In focused freewriting, the emphasis is on writing…*anything*…without worrying about whether what you put down is even vaguely related to your topic. The key is just to start writing—a diary entry, the biography of your dog, your thoughts about current rock videos—and *not to stop* until the time is up.

Brainstorming is useful when you are ready to write but just can't get a handle on exactly where to begin. Freewriting is useful when you can't get your brain to work at all. Both methods will help you start writing, which is all you are trying to do.

Document Your Sources

To avoid plagiarism, you must document the source when you put any of the following in your paper:

- Quotations taken from a published source.
- Someone else's theories or ideas.
- Someone else's sentences, phrases, or special expressions.
- Facts, figures, and research data compiled by someone else.
- Graphs, pictures, and charts designed by someone else.

There are some exceptions. You don't need to document the source of a fact, theory, or expression that is common knowledge. And you also do not need a source note when you use a phrase or expression for which there is no known author.

To judge whether a statement needs a source note, ask yourself whether readers would otherwise think that you had come up with the information or idea all by yourself. If the answer is yes, you need a source note. If you're in doubt, include a source note anyway.

Footnotes

For many years, the preferred way to credit sources was the footnote. Two other forms of documentation, endnotes and parenthetical notes, are popular now as well.

A footnote is a source note that appears at the bottom of a page of text. You put a raised (superscript) number at the end of the statement or fact you need to document, which tells your readers to look at the bottom of the page for a note about the source of the data.

What goes in a footnote? The same information that's in the bibliography listing. *And* the exact page number the information appears on.

In front of that source note, you put the same superscript number as you put next to the statement or fact in your text.

There is no limit to the number of footnotes you may have in your paper. Number each footnote consecutively, starting with the number 1. For every footnote "flag" in your paper, be sure there is a corresponding source note at the bottom of the page.

Like bibliography listings, different authorities cite different rules for setting up footnotes. Ask your teacher whose rules you are to follow.

If your teacher doesn't have a preference, you might as well use the MLA rules, which I use as well. Also, be sure to refer to *Improve Your Writing* for a more in-depth examination of source documentation.

(The MLA guidelines are used primarily for papers in the arts and humanities. If you are doing a paper for a physical or social science class, check with your teacher or professor as to which style you are to follow. Specific— and different—style sheets are used in biology, chemistry, math, physics, engineering, psychology, and so forth.)

Step 8: Do Additional Research

Did you discover any gaps in your research as you put together your first draft? Raise some questions that you need additional information to answer? If so, now's the time to head for the library for one last crack at the books.

Step 9: Write the Second Draft

The goal for this phase is to edit for meaning—improve the flow of your paper, organize your thoughts better, clarify confusing points, and strengthen weak arguments.

As you review your rough draft, ask yourself the following questions:

- Do your thoughts move logically from one point to the next?
- Is the meaning of every sentence and paragraph crystal clear?
- Does every sentence make a point—or support one?
- Do you move smoothly from one paragraph to the next? Or do you jump randomly from one topic to another?

- Do you support your conclusions with solid evidence—research data, examples, statistics?

- Do you include a good *mix* of evidence—quotes from experts, scientific data, personal experiences, historical examples?

- Do you have a solid introduction and conclusion?

- Did you write in your own words and style? Or have you merely strung together phrases and quotes "borrowed" from other authors?

- Have you explained your subject thoroughly, or assumed that readers have more knowledge about it than they actually might? (Remember: *You're* familiar with the topic now, but just because something is now obvious to you doesn't mean your readers will know what you're talking about.)

- Have you convinced your readers that your thesis is valid?

- Is there any information that, while correct and informative, just doesn't belong? Cut it out!

- Have you maintained a consistent point of view (i.e., first, second, or third person throughout)?

- Does your last paragraph successfully summarize the entire paper and effectively "close" your argument?

Mark any trouble spots with a colored pencil or pen. If you have an idea on how to fix a section, jot it down on your rough draft. Now sit down and begin to rewrite. Focus on all of those problem areas you found. If necessary, add new information. Play with sentences, paragraphs, even entire sections.

Rework Your Opening and Closing Paragraphs

When you feel you have created a wonderful paper, examine your opening and closing paragraphs. Take the time to go over these—again and again—to make them the best you possibly can. More than one "okay-not-great" paper has earned a better-than-expected grade because of an "A+" introduction and conclusion.

Your paper's opening paragraph is the most important of all. It sets out what you will be arguing for or against (and why you chose that side) and introduces the rest of the paper. If it's well written, it will seamlessly lead your teacher into the rest of the paper *and* earn you points for solid organization. If it's poorly written, it may not matter what follows—your teacher may conclude you obviously don't know what you're talking about and grade accordingly (while spending less time than he might have otherwise on the rest of the paper).

Think of the introduction and the conclusion as the bread in a sandwich, with the information in between as the hamburger, lettuce, tomato, and pickle. The main attraction may be what's between the slices, but you need the bread to even call it a sandwich.

Here are some ways to start off your paper with a little zing:

- Say something that grabs attention.
- Say something controversial.
- Paint a picture of a scene.
- Recreate an event.
- Use a potent quote.
- Ask a provocative question.

But don't—absolutely do *not*—use a joke. The joke will be on you. Most teachers have no sense of humor once they start grading papers (presuming they did before).

Check All Your Facts

When you finish editing for content and meaning, print or type a clean copy of your paper, then double-check all of your facts for accuracy:

- Did you spell names, terms, and places correctly?
- When you quoted dates and statistics, did you get your numbers straight?
- Do you have a source note (or preliminary source note) for every fact, expression, or idea that is not your own?
- If you quoted material from a source, did you quote that source exactly, word for word, comma for comma, and did you put the material in quotation marks?

Mark any corrections on your new draft. Again, use a colored pen or pencil so you can easily spot corrections later.

Keep Rewriting

Now take an even closer look at your sentences and paragraphs. Try to make them smoother, tighter, and easier to understand:

- Use action verbs and the active voice: "Some apes in captivity have survived for 30 or more years" is better than "Ages of 30 years or more have been enjoyed by some apes in captivity."
- Consider dropping constructions beginning with "there is (was)" from your vocabulary: "There was a storm at sea" is a tired and boring way to proclaim, "A storm raged."
- Is there too much fat? Seize every opportunity to make the same point in fewer words.

- Are there places where phrasing or construction is awkward? Try to rearrange the sentence or section so that it flows better.

- Did you use descriptive, colorful words? Did you tell your reader, "The planes were damaged," or paint a more colorful and creative picture: "The planes were broken-down hulks of rusted metal— bullet-ridden, neglected warbirds that could barely limp down the runway"?

- Consult a thesaurus for synonyms that work better than the words you originally chose. But don't get carried away and use words so obscure that the average reader wouldn't know their meaning. When in doubt, opt for the familiar word rather than the obscure, the shorter vs. the longer, the tangible vs. the hypothetical, the direct word vs. the roundabout phrase.

- Have you overused cliches or slang expressions? Especially in academic writing, neither are particularly appreciated. Your paper may be "dead as a doornail" if you don't "get the lead out," get rid of some of the "oldies but goodies," and make sure your paper is "neat as a pin."

- Have you overused particular words? Constantly using the same words makes your writing boring. Check a thesaurus for other possibilities.

- How do the words *sound*? When you read your paper aloud, does it flow like a rhythmic piece of music? Or plod along like a funeral dirge?

- One of the best ways to give your writing a little "oomph" is to vary your sentence structure. Use short sentences occasionally. Even very short. Without subjects. Use simple sentences, complex sentences (an independent clause and one or more dependent clauses), and embedded sentences (combining two clauses using relative pronouns rather than conjunctions). And despite what Mrs. Dougherty taught you in eighth grade, it really *is* okay to start sentences with "and" or "but." And to use sentence fragments for emphasis and effect. Really.

- Always remember the point of the paper: to communicate your ideas as clearly and concisely as possible. So don't get lost in the details. If you have to choose between that "perfect" word and the most organized paper imaginable, opt for the latter.

Again, mark corrections on your draft with a colored pen or pencil. No need to reprint your paper yet—unless it's gotten so marked up that it's hard to read!

Step 10: Prepare Your Final Bibliography

Your bibliography should be at the end of your paper, on a separate page or pages:

- One inch from the top of the page: Center the title "Works Cited" or "Works Consulted," depending upon which type of bibliography you're doing.

- Use the same margins as you did for the rest of your paper— one inch all the way around.

- Treat your bibliography pages as if they are a continuation of the text of your paper and number them accordingly— *don't* start repaginating.

- List sources alphabetically, by the author's last name. If no author is given, list by the first word in the title of the work (unless the first word is "A," "An," or "The," in which case list by the second word of the title).

- The first line of each listing should be flush with the left margin. Indent all other lines five spaces from the left margin.

- Double-space all listings and double-space between entries.

- Abbreviate all months except May, June, and July.

Step 11: Check Your Spelling and Proofread

It's time to rid your paper of any mistakes in grammar and spelling.

I've told you your thoughts are the most important element of your paper. And they are. But it's also true that glaring mistakes in grammar and spelling will lead your teacher to believe that you are either careless or downright ignorant—neither of which will bode well for your final grade.

So get out your dictionary and a reference book on English usage and grammar. Scour your paper, sentence by sentence, marking corrections with your colored pen or pencil. Look for:

- **Misspelled words.** Check every word. If you're using a spellchecking computer program, be careful of sound-alike words. "There" might be spelled correctly, but not if you meant to write "their."

- **Incorrect punctuation.** Review the rules for placement of commas, quotation marks, periods, and other punctuation. Make sure you follow those rules throughout your paper.

- **Incorrect sentence structure.** Look for dangling participles, split infinitives, sentences that end in prepositions, and other various grammar no-no's.

Step 12: Have Someone *Else* Proofread

Reprint your paper, making all those corrections you marked during the last step. Format the paper according to the teacher's instructions. Incorporate your final footnotes and bibliography.

Give your paper a title, one that's as short and sweet as possible but tells readers what they can expect to learn from your paper.

Find someone who is a good proofreader—a parent, relative, friend— and ask him or her to proofread your paper before you put together the final draft.

Steps 13–15: The Final Draft

Incorporate any changes or errors your proofreader may have caught. Print the final draft. Proof it again—very carefully.

Here are a couple of tricks of the trade: 1) *Read your paper aloud*. Go ahead—shout it from the rooftops! It's amazing how easily you'll discover misplaced words, poor grammar, even a misspelling or two. 2) *Read your paper backwards*. This forces you to focus on each individual word and is a sensational way to pick up misspellings.

Last step? Put your paper in a new manuscript binder or folder. Then, turn it in—on time, of course!

Oral Reports

There are some key differences between writing a report and pre- senting it orally, especially if you don't want to make the mistake of just reading your report in front of the class.

If you've been assigned to give a talk for a class, it will probably fall into one of the following categories:

- **Exposition:** a straightforward statement of facts.
- **Argument:** trying to change the opinions of at least a portion of the audience.
- **Description:** providing a visual picture to your listeners.
- **Narration:** storytelling.

The most common forms of oral reports assigned in school will be exposition and argument. You'll find that you will research and organize information for these types of speeches pretty much the way you would a term paper.

A note of caution: If you're preparing an *argument*, don't convince yourself you don't have to research *both* sides of the topic just because you're only presenting *one* of them. You should be doubly prepared with all the facts, as you might be challenged with questions or the arguments of other speakers.

As you gather information for your report, making notes on index cards as you did for your term paper, keep this in mind: In order for you to be effective, you must use some different techniques when you *tell* your story rather than *write* it. Here are a few:

- **Don't make your topic too broad.** This advice, offered for preparing written reports as well, is even more important when preparing a talk. Try giving an effective speech on "Eleanor Roosevelt," "Jane Austen's novels," or "The U.S. military" in 15 minutes, frequently the amount of time assigned for oral reports. These topics are more suited to a series of books!

"How Eleanor Roosevelt changed the role of First Lady," "The way the movie *Clueless* failed to meet the standards set by Austen's *Emma*," or "The pros and cons of inoculating all military personnel with the anthrax vaccine" are more manageable topics. Narrowing the scope of your talk will help you research and organize it more effectively.

- **Don't overuse statistics.** While they're very important for lending credibility to your position, too many will only weigh down your speech and bore your audience.

- **Anecdotes add color and life to your talk.** But use them sparingly, because they can slow down your speech. Get to the punch line before the yawns start.

- **Be careful with quotes.** Unlike a term paper, a speech allows you to establish yourself as an authority with less fear of being accused of plagiarism. So you can present a lot more facts without attribution. (But you'd better have the sources in case you're asked about your facts.) You can use quotes, though, when they contain distinctive language or elicit an emotion. Be sure to attribute the source.

I've found that trying to shuffle a bunch of papers in front of a class is difficult. Note cards that fit in the palm of your hand are a lot easier to use, but only if the notes on them are very short and to the point. Then they act as "triggers" rather than verbatim cue cards. The shorter the notes— and the more often you practice your report so each note triggers the right information—the more effective your report will be. (And the less you will have to look at them, making eye contact with your class and teacher easier.)

Here are ways to make oral reports more effective:

- Pick out one person to talk to—preferably a friend, but any animated and/or interested person will do—and direct your talk at him or her.

- Practice, practice, *practice* your presentation. Jangled nerves are often the result of a lack of confidence. The more confident you are that you know your material, the less nervous you will be, and the better and more spontaneous your presentation will be.

- If you are like me and suffer from involuntary "shakes" at the mere thought of standing in front of a roomful of people, make sure you can use a lectern, desk, or something to cling to.

Take a deep breath before you go to the front of the class. And don't worry about pausing, even taking another deep breath or two, if you lose your place or find your confidence slipping away.

If every trick in the world still doesn't calm you down, consider taking a public speaking course (Dale Carnegie, *et al*), joining the Toastmasters Club, or seeking out similar extracurricular help.

Chapter 8

How to Study for Tests

Throughout your educational life—and, more than likely, the rest of your life—testing will be an inevitable if sometimes frightening and distressing reality. The sooner you learn the techniques of preparing for, taking, and mastering tests, the better off you'll be.

What Do They Want to Know?

Many tests are as much a measure of the *way* you study— your ability to organize a mountain of material—as they are a measure of your knowledge of the material itself. This is especially true of any test that purports to measure knowledge spread across the years and your mastery of a broad spectrum of material—the SAT; GRE; bar or medical exam; exams for nurses, CPAs, financial planners, etc.; and others. Which means the better you *study*, the better your *score* will probably be on such tests.

Before you can decide *how* to study for a particular test, it's imperative that you know exactly what you're being tested *on*. Preparing for a weekly quiz is far different than preparing for a final exam. And the biggest final of your life is child's play compared to "monster tests" like the oral exams I faced before they allowed me to graduate college—which covered everything I was supposed to have learned in four years.

Studying for a standardized test like the PSAT, SAT, ACT, or GRE is also completely different—you can't pull out your textbook and, knowing what chapters are being included, just "bone up."

The structure of the test is also of paramount importance, not necessarily in terms of how you study, but how you tackle it once you get your test book.

What Are You Afraid Of?

Tests are scary creatures. So before I start doling out test-taking techniques, let's tackle one of the key problems many of you will face: test anxiety, a reaction characterized by sweaty palms, a blank mind, and the urge to flee to Pago Pago on the next available cargo ship.

What does it mean when someone proclaims they don't "test well?" For many, it really means they don't *study* well (or, at the very least, prepare well). For others, it could mean they are easily distracted, unprepared for the *type* of test they are confronting, or simply unprepared mentally to take *any* test.

We all recognize the competitive nature of tests. Some of us rise to the occasion when facing such a challenge. Others are thrown off balance by the pressure. Both reactions probably have little to do with one's level of knowledge, relative intelligence, or amount of preparation. The smartest students in your class may be the ones most afraid of tests.

Believe Me, You're Not Alone

Take heart—very few people look forward to a test; more of you are afraid of tests than you'd think. But that doesn't mean you have to fear them.

Few people enter a testing site cool, calm, and ready for action. Most of us have various butterflies gamboling in our stomachs, sweat glands operating in overdrive, and a sincere desire to be somewhere else… *anywhere* else.

The more pressure you put on yourself—the larger you allow a test (and, of course, your hoped-for good scores) to loom in your own mind—the less you are helping yourself. (And the bigger the test really *is*, the more likely you are to keep reminding yourself of its importance.)

Let's face it: Your scores on some tests *can* have a major effect on where you go to college, whether you go to graduate school, or whether you get the job you want. But no matter how important a test may be to your career, it is just as important to *deemphasize* that test's importance in your mind. This should have no effect on your preparation—you should still study as if your life depended on a superior score. It might!

Keeping the whole experience in perspective might also help: Twenty years from now, nobody will remember, or care, what you scored on *any* test—no matter how life-determining you feel that test is right now.

Of course, you *can* make it easier to do all this by *not* going out of your way—certainly before an especially big or important test— to add *more* stress to an already stressful event. Two days before the SAT is *not* the time to dump a boyfriend, move, change jobs, take out a big loan, or create any other waves in your normally placid river of life.

With Friends Like These...

Some people thrive on their own misery and are jealous if you don't feed on it, too. They want to suck you into their gloom, whether you really know or care what's happening.

These Anxiety Professionals are the people to avoid when you're preparing for an exam. "Oh, I'll never learn all this stuff!" they cry. You might not win points with Miss Manners by saying, "If you'd shut up and study, you might!" But you *can* have the pleasure of *thinking* it—on your way to a quiet place to study alone.

Watch out for those "friends" who call you the night before the exam to wail, "I just found out we have to know Chapter 12!" Don't fall into their trap. Instead of dialing 911, calmly remind them that the printed sheet the professor passed out two weeks ago clearly says that the test will cover Chapters 6 through 11. Then hang up, get on with your life, and let them wring their hands all the way to the bottom of the grading sheet. (Of course, if *you* don't bother to check what's going to be on the test, a call like this *will* panic you...and waste your time.)

How to Lower Your AQ (Anxiety Quotient)

To come to terms with the "importance" of a test, read the following list. Knowing the answers to as many of these questions as possible will help reduce your anxiety:

1. What material will the exam cover?
2. How many total points are possible?
3. What will this exam count for?
4. How much time will I have to take the exam?
5. Where will the exam be held?

6. What kinds of questions will be on the exam (matching, multiple-choice, essay, true/false, and so forth)?

7. How many of each type of question will be on the exam?

8. How many points will be assigned to each question?

9. Will certain sections of the test count more than others?

10. Will it be an open-book exam?

11. What can I take in with me? Calculator? Candy bar? Other material crucial to my success?

12. Will I be penalized for wrong answers?

Hit the Road, Jack

To shake off pretest anxiety, take a walk or a vigorous swim. In the days before an exam, no matter how "big" it is, don't study too hard or too much, or you'll walk into the exam with a fried brain.

You've already found that scheduling breaks during your study routine makes it easier for you to focus on your books and complete your assignments faster and with more concentration. Scheduling breaks during test preparation has the same effect.

No matter what the time limits or pressures, don't feel you cannot afford such a brief respite. You may need it *most* when you're convinced you can *least* afford it, just as those who most need time-management techniques "just don't have the time" to learn them.

Relax Already

If your mind is a jumble of facts and figures, names and dates, you may find it difficult to zero in on the specific details you need to recall, even if you know all the material backwards and forwards. The adrenaline rushing through your system may just make "instant retrieval" impossible.

The simplest relaxation technique is deep breathing. Lean back in your chair, relax your muscles, and take three very deep breaths (count to 10 while you hold each one).

There are a variety of meditation techniques that may also work for you. Each is based on a similar principle— focusing your mind on one thing to the exclusion of everything else. While you're concentrating on the object of your meditation (even if the object is nothing, a nonsense word, or a spot on the wall), your mind can't be thinking about anything else, which allows it to slow down a bit.

The next time you can't focus, try sitting back, taking three deep breaths, and concentrating for a minute or two on the word "Ron." When you're done, you should be in a far more relaxed state and ready to tackle any test.

Preparing for Great Test Scores

Some rites of preparation are pertinent to any test, from a weekly quiz to the SAT, and everything in between.

Plan Ahead

I admit it. When I was a student, even in college, my attention span tended to be bounded by weekends. Tell me in October that there'd be a big test the first week of December and I'd remember, oh, around November 30th.

Of such habits are cramming, crib sheets, and failing marks made.

The key to avoiding all of these unpleasantries is regular, *periodic review*. The more often you review, the less often you will have to pull all-nighters the week of the test. You already will have stayed on top of the material, written down and asked questions that arose from your reviews, and gone over class and textbook notes to make sure you understand everything. Your last-minute review will be relatively leisurely and organized, not feverish and harried.

Use Two Alarm Clocks

Doing poorly on a test is discouraging. Failing a test you felt ready for is depressing. Missing the test entirely is devastating. It's imperative that you know when and where all tests are scheduled and allow ample time to get to them.

If you're still in high school, getting to a particular test shouldn't be too hard—it will probably be held during your regular class period in your normal classroom. But in college, tests may be scheduled at hours different than the normal class period...and at entirely different sites.

Likewise, major tests like the PSAT and SAT may not even be held at your school. In such cases, make sure you allow enough time to drive to, or be driven to, wherever you have to be—especially if you're not quite sure how to get there!

As soon as you know the time and location of a test, enter it on your weekly calendar. Whether in high school, college, or grad school, most schools set aside a week, two, or even more for final exams. This exam period is usually clearly marked in your college handbook, announced in class (usually on the first day), and printed on your class syllabus.

If you have an upcoming exam early in the morning and you are afraid you won't be in shape for it, do a bit of subterfuge on your body and brain—get up early for several days before the exam, have a good breakfast, and do homework or review your notes. This will help jump-start your brain and get it used to the idea of solving equations or thinking seriously about Shakespeare at an earlier-than-usual hour.

Make Optional Assignments Mandatory

Sometimes, in addition to your regular reading and other assignments, the teacher will assign optional reading at the beginning of a course. These books, articles, and monographs may never be discussed in any class—but material from them may be included on a test, especially a final exam. If you have neglected to add this supplementary reading to your regular calendar, but wish to read them before the test, make sure you allow enough time to buy or find these books. A lot of other students may have also left such reading to the last minute, and you may be unable to find the material you need if you wait too long.

Pens, Pencils...a Candy Bar

Lastly, bring to the test whatever materials you need, from pens and pencils to calculators. I also recommend— especially for a long test like the SAT or ACT—that you have a candy bar, hard candies, granola bar, or some other "quick energy" snack to munch when you need to give yourself a figurative slap in the face.

Although many testing booklets will include room for notes, it may not be sufficient for your purposes. If you are asked to write three, five, or even more essay questions, you will want a lot of scratch paper to outline and organize your thoughts before you put pen to paper. Likewise, a particularly complex math test may quickly use up every square inch of margin, so bring along a separate writing tablet or even a stack of scrap paper. There are few situations in which their use won't be allowed.

If You Didn't Listen Before...

Review, review, review. If you don't follow my advice for periodic review, set aside the time to review and study a week or two before the test. Most colleges—and many high schools—offer a reading or study period, usually the week before midterms or finals, when no classes are offered. Library hours are often extended. Take advantage of this time.

The more material you need to review, the more important it is to clear your schedule. A four-, five- or six-course load covering 20, 40, or more books, lectures and discussions, papers, and projects will easily generate hundreds of pages of notes. Reviewing, understanding, and studying them will require your full-time effort for a week, even two. So make sure all other end-of-term work, especially major projects and papers, are out of the way.

Organize Your Material

1. Gather all the material you have been using for the course: books, workbooks, handouts, notes, homework, and previous tests and papers.

2. Compare the contents with the material you will be tested on and ask yourself: What exactly do I need to review for this test?

3. Select the material for review. Reducing the pile of books and papers will be a psychological aid—it'll seem as if you have more than enough time and energy to study for the test.

4. Photocopy and complete the Pretest Organizer at the end of this chapter. Consider carefully the "Material to be covered" section. Be specific. The more detailed you are, the better job you'll do reviewing all the areas that you should know. This exercise will help you *quantify* what you need to do.

5. As you review the material and conclude that you know it for the test, put a bold check mark on the "Review" line.

6. Hot tip: Make a crib sheet as if you were going to cheat on the test, which, of course, you are not. Use it for last-minute review. And if you are lucky enough to get an open-book test, thank me!

Allocate the Time You Need

Consider these questions when figuring out the time you need to allocate to study for a particular test:

- **How much time do I usually spend studying for this type of exam?** What have been the results? If you usually spend three hours and you consistently get Ds, perhaps you need to reassess the time you're spending or, more accurately, *mis*spending.

- **What grade do I have going for me now?** If it's a solid B and you're convinced you can't get an A, you may decide to devote *less* time to this test and more to a subject in which you have a better shot at a top grade. If you have a C+ and a good grade on the exam would give you a solid B, you may decide to devote more time to *this* subject.

- **What special studying do I have to do?** It's one thing to review notes and practice with a study group, but if you need to sit in a language lab and listen to hours of tapes or run the slower group of gerbils through the alphabet once more, plan accordingly.

- **Organize the materials you need to study, pace yourself, and check to see how much material you have covered in the first hour of review.** How does this compare to what you have left to study? Not every hour will be equally productive, but you should be able to project the time you need based on what you are able to accomplish in an hour.

Why Cramming Doesn't Work

We've all done it at one time or another, with one excuse or another—waited until the last minute and then tried to cram a week's or month's or entire semester's worth of work into a single night or weekend. Did it work for you? Didn't think so.

The reality is that cramming works—on one level—for a small minority of students. Somehow, they're able to shove more "stuff" into short-term memory than the rest of us and actually remember it, at least for 24 hours. After those 24 hours? Gone with the wind. Which means if they managed to do well on a weekly quiz, all that cramming didn't do them a bit of good for the upcoming midterm or final.

The rest of us don't even get that smidgen of good news—after a night of no sleep and too much coffee, we're lucky if we remember where the test *is* the next morning. A couple of hours later, trying to stay awake long enough to make it back to bed, we not only haven't learned anything, we haven't even done very well on the test we crammed for!

That's probably the best reason of all not to cram—it just doesn't work!

How to Cram Anyway

Nevertheless, despite your resolve, best intentions, and firm conviction that cramming is a losing proposition, you may well find yourself—though hopefully not too often— in the position of needing to do *something* the night before a test you haven't studied for at all. If so, here's some advice that will make your night of cramming at least marginally successful:

Be realistic about what you can do. You absolutely *cannot* master an entire semester's worth of work in a single night, especially if your class attendance has been sporadic (or nonexistent) and you've skimmed two books out of a syllabus of two dozen. The *more* information you try to cram in, the *less* effective you will be.

Being realistic means soberly assessing your situation— you're hanging by your thumbs and are just trying to avoid falling into the boiling oil. Avoiding the oil, saving the damsel in distress, and inheriting the kingdom ("acing" the test) is a bit too much to ask for, no matter whom your Fairy Godmother is.

Be selective and study in depth. The more classes you've managed to miss, the more selective you need to be in organizing your cram session. You *can't* study it all. So you must identify—as best you can—what topics you are sure will be on the test. Then study *only those*. It's better in this case to know a lot about a little rather than a little about a lot. You may get lucky and pick the three topics the three essays cover!

Massage your memory. Use every memory technique you've learned (and the additional ones in *Improve Your Memory*) to maximize what you're able to retain in your short-term memory.

Know when to give up. When you can't remember your name or focus on the book in front of you, give up and get some sleep.

Consider an early morning rather than a late-night cram, especially if you're a "morning" person. I've found it more effective to go to bed and get up early rather than go to bed late and get up exhausted.

Spend the first few minutes of the test writing down whatever you remember but are afraid you'll forget.

When in Doubt, Ask

Yes, there are teachers who test you on the most mundane details of their course, requiring you to review every book, every note, every scribble.

I don't think most teachers work that way. You will more than likely be tested on some subset of the course— those particular topics or problems or facts or figures the teacher believes most important.

How do you know what those are? To put it bluntly, how do you know what's going to be on the test?

Teachers give many clues. In general, the more often you see or hear the same material, the more important it probably is and the more likely it is that it will show up on a test.

A fact or topic need not be repeated in order to scream "Learn me!" Just as you learned to watch a teacher's body language and listen for verbal clues to identify noteworthy topics, you'll learn to identify topics the teacher indicates— nonverbally—are the most important. Your teacher's attitude *toward* note taking may tip you off, as well. If he or she requires you to take detailed notes—even wants them turned in (sometimes in high school, rarely in college)—I'd figure that your class notes are far and away more important than the textbook(s). Study accordingly.

Have you saved earlier tests and quizzes from that class? Returned exams, especially if they contain a lot of comments from your teacher, should give you an excellent indication of where to concentrate your study time.

Is it wrong to ask the teacher what kind of test to expect? Absolutely not. Will he or she always tell you? Absolutely not. If you have access to old exams written by the same teacher, especially if they cover the same material you're going to be tested on, use *them* for review.

Don't expect the same questions to appear again. No teacher is *that* accommodating. But the way the test is prepared, the kinds of questions employed, and the mix of questions (100 true/false, 50 multiple-choice, and one—count 'em—one essay) will give a much better idea of what to expect on your test.

And see if you can find anyone who had this teacher last year or last semester. Can they give you any advice, tips, hints, or warnings?

Some teachers love one type of question. Some are true/false freaks; others push the multiple-choice/short answer combo. If old tests, former students, the teacher's own comments on the test coming up, and your own experience tell you this is true, you might as well study for that kind of test. You still have to know the material, of course. It's just that you may need to remind yourself that you're going to have to deal with it in a particular fashion.

The best teachers use a combination of test questions to find out what you know. Frankly, some of them hate grading essay questions, so they rarely use them. Why do other teachers choose essay questions?

1. They are quicker and easier to prepare.
2. They may be preferred when a group is small and the test will not be reused.
3. They are used to explore students' attitudes rather than measure their achievements.
4. They are used to encourage and reward the development of the students' skill in writing.
5. They are suitable when it's important for the students to explain or describe.
6. They are more suitable to some material. You're likely to have more essay questions in English and history than you are in the sciences.

Some teachers prefer objective questions because:

1. They are preferred when the group is large and the test may be reused.
2. They are more efficient when highly reliable test scores must be obtained quickly.
3. They are more suitable for covering a larger amount of content in the same amount of time.
4. They are easier for the teacher to give an impartial grade. Every student has to write down "C" to get number 22 correct.
5. They are easier for some teachers to create.
6. They may be used when students need to demonstrate or show.

Never Study "Everything"

Once you've discovered the type of test facing you, you need to figure out what's going to be *on* it (and hence, what you need to study). Remember, it's rarely, if ever, "everything."

At most, do a cursory review of material you are convinced is simply not important enough to be included on an upcoming test. This will automatically give you more time to concentrate on those areas you're sure *will* be included.

Then create a "To Study" sheet for each test. On it, list specific books to review, notes to recheck, and topics, principles, ideas, and concepts to go over. This method will minimize procrastination, logically organize your studying, and give you ongoing "jolts" of accomplishment as you complete each item.

Test Yourself

Just as you have made it a habit to write down questions as you study your texts, why not try to construct your own tests? The harder you make them, the better prepared and more confident you will be when you confront the real test.

Practice tests offer some real advantages, whether you're studying for a weekly quiz, the SAT, or your bar exam. In fact, the longer and more "standardized" the test, the more important it is to be familiar with its structure, rules, and traps.

First and foremost, familiarization with whatever type of test you're taking is vitally important, as it enables you to strategically study the material (prioritize) and strategically attack the test (organize). Familiarization breeds comfort and being comfortable—*relaxed*—is a key component to doing well.

Familiarization also breeds organization, allowing you to concentrate on the test itself and not on its structure. This gives you more time to actually *take* the test rather than figure it out. It also reduces the effect of whatever time restraints the test imposes on you.

Last but not least, taking practice tests is a highly effective way to study and remember the material.

Test-Day Rules and Reminders

If the test is not simply during a regular class period, make sure to arrive at the test site early. Based on your preferences (from Chapter 2), sit where you like.

Be careful, however. There may be some variations you have to take into account. In a test where there are 200 or 300 people in a room, there is a distinct advantage to sitting up front: You can hear the instructions and the answers to questions better, and you generally get the test first (and turn it in last).

Take the Time to Skim the Test

If you have permission to go all the way through it, do so before you even start testing. Give yourself an overview of what lies ahead. That way you can spot the easier sections and get an idea of the point values assigned to each section.

I know students who look through the entire test and break it down into time segments before they read any question or write a single answer—allocating 20 minutes for section one, 40 for section two, and so forth. Even on multiple-choice tests, they count the total number of questions, divide by the time allotted, and set "goals" on what time they should reach question 10, question 25, and so on.

Know the Ground Rules

Will you be penalized for guessing? The teacher may inform you that you will earn two points for every correct answer, but lose one point for every incorrect one. This will certainly affect whether you guess or skip the question—or, at the very least, how many potential answers you feel you need to eliminate before the odds of guessing are in your favor. (As far as the SAT is concerned, there isn't a penalty for guessing, so don't leave an answer blank!)

In the case of a standardized test like the SAT, ACT, or GRE, read the instructions on a previous test before you go to the test site. (There are numerous books that include "actual tests" in their prep books.) Then just skim the instructions in your booklet or on the computer to make sure nothing has changed. It will save you minutes—time that is precious indeed during any such test.

Are the questions or sections weighted? Some tests may have two, three, or more sections, some of which count for very little—10 or 15 percent of your final score. One part, usually a major essay, may be more heavily weighted—50 percent or more of your grade. Let this influence the amount of time and energy you devote to each section.

Beware of time. Again, if questions or sections are weighted, you will want to allow extra time for those that count for 90 percent of the score and whip through the 10-percent section as the teacher is collecting booklets.

Draw Your Way to a Good Score

Throughout a test, don't miss an opportunity to draw a picture for yourself if it helps you understand the question or figure out the right answer. If the question deals with any sort of cause-and-effect that has several steps in it, draw or write down those steps very quickly, using abbreviated words or symbols. This may help you see missing pieces, understand relationships between parts, and select the right answer.

Discriminate and Eliminate

There is usually nothing wrong with guessing, unless, of course, you know wrong answers will be penalized. Even then, the question is how *often* to guess (and on what basis).

If there's no penalty for wrong answers, you should *never* leave an answer blank. But you should also do everything you can to increase your odds of getting it right. If every multiple-choice question gives you four possible answers, you have a 25-percent chance of being right (and, of course, a 75-percent chance of being wrong) each time you have to guess.

But if you can eliminate a single answer—one you are reasonably certain cannot be right—your chances of being correct increase to 33 percent.

And, of course, if you can get down to a choice between two answers, it's just like flipping a coin: 50-50. In the long run, you will guess as many right as wrong. Even if there is a penalty for guessing, I would probably pick one answer if I had managed to reduce the odds to 50-50.

Presuming that you've managed to eliminate one or more answers, but are still unsure of the correct answer and have no particular way to eliminate any others, here are some real insider tips to make your "guesses" more educated:

- If two answers sound alike, choose neither.
- The most "obvious" answer to a difficult question is probably wrong, but an answer that is close to it is probably right.
- If the answers that are left to a mathematical question cover a broad range, eliminate the extremes and choose a number in the middle.
- If two quantities are very close, choose one of them.

- If two numbers differ only by a decimal point (and the others aren't close), choose one of them. (Example: 2.3, 40, 1.5, 6, 15; I'd go with 1.5 or 15. If I could at least figure out from the question where the decimal point should go, even better!)

- If two answers to a mathematical problem *look* alike—either formulas or shapes—choose one of them.

Remember: This is not the way to ace a test—these are just some tried-and-true ways to increase your guessing power when *you have absolutely nothing else to go on*.

Should You Ever Change a Guess?

How valid was your first guess? It was probably pretty darned good (presuming you had some basis for guessing in the first place). So good that you should *only* change it *if*:

- It really was just a wild guess and, upon further thought, you conclude that answer actually should be eliminated (in which case your next guess is, at least, not quite so wild).

- You remembered something that changed the odds of your guess completely (or the answer to a later question helped you figure out the answer to this one!).

- You miscalculated on a math problem.

- You misread the question and didn't notice a "not," "always," or other important qualifier.

What if you eliminate four of the five answers and are convinced that the one that's left—your supposedly "right" answer—is flat-out wrong? Eliminate *it* and start your analysis again with the other four answers.

If you do guess at any of the objective questions and expect that your test paper will be returned to you, place a little dot or other symbol beside them. That way you will be able to assess how successful your guessing was.

If there is time during a test for you to come back to questions and think about them one more time, go ahead and cross out the answers you know aren't correct. That will simply save you time. You will ignore the answers that are struck out and concentrate on the ones that remain. A small point, but it can save you several seconds per question.

When you think you have finished a whole section, double-check to make sure you really have. Look on the answer sheet or in the blue book to make sure all the questions have been answered.

You *Will* Follow the Instructions!

Read and understand the directions. If you're supposed to check off every correct answer to each question in a multiple-choice test—and you're assuming only one answer to each question is correct—you're going to miss a lot of answers!

If you're to pick one essay question out of three, or two out of five, you will almost certainly run out of time if you try to answer every one. Even if you do manage to complete all five, the teacher will probably only grade the first two. Because you allocated so much time to the other three, it's highly doubtful your first two answers will be detailed and polished enough to earn a good grade.

If there are pertinent facts or formulas you're afraid you'll forget, write them down somewhere in your test booklet before you do anything else. It won't take much time, and it could save you some serious memory jogs later.

Whom Are You Impressing on Your Way Out?

Leave time at the end to recheck your answers, and *don't* make a habit of leaving tests early. There is little to be gained from supposedly impressing the teacher and other students with how smart you (think you) are by being first to finish. Take the time to make sure you've done your best. If you are completely satisfied with your answers to all of the questions, it's fine to leave, even if you are first. But in general, slowing down will help you avoid careless mistakes.

Likewise, don't worry about what everybody else is doing. Even if you're the last person left, who cares? Everybody else could have failed, no matter how early and confidently they strode from the room! So take all the time you need and do the best you can.

16 Tips for "Acing" Multiple-Choice Tests

1. Read the question in full before you look at any of the answers. Come up with your own answer before examining any of the choices.

2. Be careful you don't read too much into questions. Don't try to second-guess the test preparer and look for patterns or tricks that aren't really there.

3. Underline the key words in a reading selection.

4. A positive choice is more likely to be correct than a negative one.

5. Don't go against your first impulse unless you are *sure* you were wrong. (Sometimes you're so smart you scare yourself.)

6. Check for negatives and other words that are there to throw you off. ("Which of the following is *not*....")

7. The answer is usually *wrong* if it contains "all," "always," "never," or "none." I repeat, usually.

8. The answer contains a great chance of being *right* if it has "sometimes," "probably," or "some."

9. When you don't know the right answer, seek out the wrong ones.

10. Don't eliminate an answer unless you actually know what every word means.

11. Don't seek out answer patterns. Just because answer "C" has appeared three times in a row doesn't mean "C" isn't the correct answer to the fourth question. Trust your knowledge.

12. Read every answer before you pick one. A sneaky test-maker will place a decoy answer that's *almost* right first, tempting you before you've even considered the other choices.

13. On a standardized test, consider transferring all the answers from one section to the answer sheet at the same time. This can save time. Just be careful: Make sure you're putting each answer in the right place.

14. The longest and/or most complicated answer to a question is often correct—the test-maker has been forced to add qualifying clauses or phrases to make that answer complete and unequivocal.

15. Be suspicious of choices that seem obvious to a two-year-old. Why would the teacher give you such a gimme? Maybe she's not, that trickster!

16. Don't give up on a question that, after one reading, seems hopelessly confusing or hard. Looking at it from another angle, restating it in your own words, or drawing a picture may help you understand it after all.

Multiple-Choice Strategy

There are three ways to attack a multiple-choice test:

1. Start at the first question and keep going, question by question, until you reach the end, never leaving a question until you have either answered it fully or made an educated guess.

2. Answer every *easy* question—the ones you know the answers to without any thinking at all or those requiring the simplest calculations—first, then go back and do the harder ones.

3. Answer the *hardest* questions first, then go back and do the easy ones.

None of these three options is inherently right or wrong. Each may work for different individuals. (And I'm assuming that these three approaches are all in the context of the test format. Weighted sections may well affect your strategy.)

The first approach is, in one sense, the quickest, in that no time is wasted reading through the whole test trying to pick out either the easiest or hardest questions. Presuming you do not allow yourself to get stumped by a single question so that you spend an inordinate amount of time on it, it is probably the method most of you employ.

The second approach ensures that you will maximize your right answers—you're putting those you are certain of down first. It may also, presuming that you knock off these easy ones relatively quickly, give you the most time to work on those that you find particularly vexing.

Many experts recommend this method because they maintain that answering so many questions one after another gives you immediate confidence to tackle the questions you're not sure about. If you find that you agree, then by all means use this strategy. However, you may consider just *noting* easy ones as you preread the test. This takes less time and, to me, delivers the same "confidence boost."

The last approach is actually the one I used. In fact, I made it a point to do the very hardest questions first, then work my way "down" the difficulty ladder. (Which means I often worked *backwards,* since many test-makers and teachers make their tests progressively more difficult.)

It may sound strange to you, so let me explain the psychology. I figured if time pressure starts getting to me at the end of the test, I would rather be in a position to answer the easiest questions—and a lot of them—in the limited time left, rather than ones I really had to think about. After all, by the end of the test, my mind was simply not working as well as it was at the beginning!

That's the major benefit of the third approach: When I was most "up," most awake, most alert, I tackled questions that required the most analysis, thinking, and interpretation. When I was most tired— near the end—I was answering the questions that were virtually "gimmes."

At the same time, I was also giving myself a *real* shot of confidence. As soon as I finished the first hard question, I already felt better. When I finished all of the hard ones, everything was downhill.

I would always, however, try to ensure adequate time to at least put down an answer for every question. Better to get one question wrong and complete three other answers than get one right and leave three blank. It is not the approach for everybody, but it may be right for you.

Don't fall into the "answer daze," that blank stare some students get when they can't think of an answer—for 10 minutes. Do *something*. Better to move on and get that one question wrong than waste invaluable time doing nothing.

All or None?

Some teachers have fallen in love with "all of the above" and "none of the above." You can't take one of their tests without those phrases appearing in every other question.

"All of the above" is often the right answer if it is an option. *Hope* that you see it as a potential answer to *every* question because *it gives you a much better chance to do better on the test* than your mastery of the material (or lack thereof) might normally warrant. Why? Because you don't have to be really sure that "all of the above" is correct to choose it. All you have to be is *pretty* sure that *two* answers are correct (and equally sure the others are not *necessarily* wrong). As long as you believe there is more than one correct answer, then "all of the above" *must* be the right choice!

Likewise, you don't have to be convinced that "none of the above" is the right answer, just *reasonably* sure that none of the other answers is absolutely correct.

Reading Comprehension Questions

This is the portion of the test where you find a short essay followed by several questions. You are supposed to find the answers to those questions in the essay. Unlike the multiple-choice questions, where the answer is actually right in front of you, the answers to the essay questions may well be hidden in one fashion or another.

Here's the method I recommend for answering comprehension questions:

1. Read the questions *before* you read the selection. They will alert you to what you're looking for and *affect the way you read the passage*. If dates are asked for, circle all dates in the passage as you read. If you're looking for facts rather than conclusions, it will, again, change the way you read the passage.

2. When you first read the question, before you look at the answers, decide what you *think* the answer is. If your answer is one of the choices, bingo!

3. If the correct answer is not obvious to you, slowly read the essay, keeping in mind the questions you've just read. Don't underline too much, but do underline conjunctions that alter the direction of the sentence: "however," "although," "nevertheless," "yet," and so forth. Because of this shift, there is a good chance that this sentence will figure in one of the questions.

   For example: "John Smith was the kind of writer who preferred writing over editing, *while* his wife Lois was interested in the latter over the former," might provide the answer to the question: "Did Lois Smith prefer writing or editing?" A careless glance back at the text will cause you to select "writing" as the answer.

4. Read the questions again. Then go back and forth, finding out the answer to the first one, the second one, and so forth. Don't skip around unless the first question is an absolute stumper. If you jump around too much, you'll get confused again and you won't answer any of the questions very completely or even correctly.

50–50 Odds Aren't Bad. True or False?

What can you do to increase your scores on true/false tests? Be more inclined to guess if you have to. After all, I encouraged you to guess on a multiple-choice test if you could eliminate enough wrong answers to get down to two, one of which is correct. Well, you're already there! So, unless you are being penalized for guessing, guess away! Even if you are being penalized, you may want to take a shot if you have the faintest clue of the correct answer.

In fact, your odds are often better than 50-50. Most test preparers tend to include more "true" statements than false. So if you really don't have any way to determine the truth of a statement, *presume it is true*. If there is a specific detail in the statement—"There are 206 bones in the adult human body"—it may also tend to be true.

Remember: For a statement to be true, *every part* of that statement must be true. Be careful of statements whose parts *are* true (or at least *may* be true), linked in such a way that the *whole* statement becomes false. Example: "Since many birds can fly, they use stones to grind their food." Many birds *do* fly, and birds *do* swallow stones to grind their food, but a *causal relationship* (the word "since") between the two clauses makes the *whole* statement false.

The longer and/or more complicated a statement in a true/false test, the less likely it's true, since every clause of it must be true (and there are so many chances for a single part of it to be false).

Be careful of double negatives: A statement claiming that something is "not uncommon" actually means that it *is* common.

Few broad, general statements are true *without exception*. So always be on your guard when you see the words "all," "always," "no," "never," "everyone," "best," "worst," "none," "nobody," or other absolutes. As long as you can think of a *single* example that proves such a statement false, then it's false. But be wary: there are statements containing such absolutes that *are* true; they are just rare. "All U.S. presidents (and/or vice presidents) have been men" is, unfortunately, all too true.

Likewise, words like "sometimes," "often," "frequently," "generally," "usually," "much," "may," "probably," "might," and "ordinarily" make more modest claims and thus usually indicate "true" statements.

Strategy tip: It's easier for a teacher to add something that makes a statement false than the other way around. So when you read it, look for anything that will make the whole statement false. If you can't find it, assume it is true.

Mastering Multiple-Choice Math

If you can avoid a calculation, it will save you time. For example, figure out the answer to the following problem *without actually doing the math*:

$281 \times 243 =$

(A) 53,762

(B) 113,428

(C) 67,283

(D) 489,593

By performing one simple task, you can eliminate two of the possible answers. Multiply the last digits in each number (1 × 3). The answer must end in 3. So (A) and (B) have been eliminated...that fast!

Now, eyeball (C) and (D). Can you find the right answer quickly? Here you are doing educated guessing, known in math circles as "guesstimating." Look: 281 × 100 is 28,100. You should be able to do that without any tools. Therefore, (D) has to be wrong. You are left with (C).

Should you do the actual math to double-check your answer? I wouldn't. You are certain that (A) and (B) are wrong. Absolutely. You know that (D) is much too high. Mark (C) as the answer and move on.

Here are other ways to better your score on math tests:

- Try to figure out what is being asked, what principles are involved, what information is important, and what's not. Don't let extraneous data throw you off track. Make sure you know the kind of answer you're seeking: Is it a speed, weight, angle, exponent, square root?

- Whenever you can, "translate" formulas and numbers into words. Estimate the answer before you even begin the actual calculation. At least you'll know the size of the ballpark you're playing in!

- Even if you're not particularly visual, pictures can often help. Try translating a particularly vexing math problem into a drawing or diagram.

- Play around. There are often different paths to the same solution, or even equally valid solutions.

- When you are checking your calculations, try working *backwards*. I've found it an easier way to catch simple arithmetical errors.

- Try to write down all of your calculations—neatly. You'll be less likely to make a mistake if you take your time, and if you *do* make a mistake, it will be a lot easier to spot.

- Show every step and formula, even if you would normally skip a few. If you knew all of the principles and formulas but miscalculated near the very beginning of your analysis, you are not going to arrive at the correct answer. *But* many enlightened math teachers will penalize you very little if they can clearly see you knew your stuff and managed to do everything right, with the exception of hitting the right button on your calculator.

- And if you are using a calculator, double-check your answer immediately. The chances of hitting *a* wrong number are high; the chances of hitting the *same* wrong number a second time are not.

There Are No "Easy" Tests

Some people think "open-book" tests are the easiest of all. They pray for them...at least until they see their first one.

These are the toughest tests of all, if only because even normally "nice" teachers feel no compunction whatsoever about making such tests as tough as a Marine drill instructor. *Heck, you can use your book!* That's like having a legal crib sheet, right? Worse yet, many open-book tests are also take-home tests, meaning you can use your notes (and any other books or tools you can think of).

Since you have to anticipate that there will be no easy questions, no matter how well you know that material, you need to do some preparation before you deal with this type of test.

- Mark important pages by turning down corners, using paper clips, or any other method that will help you quickly flip to important charts, tables, summaries, or illustrations.

- Write an index of the pages you've turned down so you know where to look immediately for a specific chart, graph, table, and so forth.

- Summarize all important facts, formulas, etc., on a separate sheet.

- If you are also allowed to bring your notes or it's a take-home test, write a brief index to your notes (general topics only) so you know where to find pertinent information.

First answer the questions for which you don't need your text. Then work on those questions on which you must rely fully on the book.

Be careful about quoting too freely from your text. Better to make up a similar example than use the same one in your book. Better to paraphrase your text than quote it directly, even if you use quotation marks.

While a take-home test is, by definition, an open-book test, it is the hardest of all. An open-book test in class simply can't last longer than the time allotted for the class. But you may be given a night or two, or even a week or longer, to complete a take-home exam.

Why are they so hard? You're *given* so much time because teachers expect that it will take you *longer* than the time available in class to finish. You may have to go well beyond your text(s) and notes even to get a handle on some of the questions, leading to some long nights. Take any *easy* eight-hour tests lately? The longer you're given, the easier it is to procrastinate ("Heck, I've got another two nights!"), and we know where *that* leads.

There are only two good aspects to balance the scales. You've certainly been given the chance to "be all that you can be." No excuse for not doing a terrific job on a test with virtually no time limit. If you tend to freeze during a normal exam, you should have far less anxiety at home in comfortable surroundings.

Writing Prize-Winning Essays

You need to budget your time for an essay test just as you should for any test—the mathematical calculations are just easier. Five questions in 50 minutes? Doesn't take an Einstein to figure out 10 minutes per essay.

Or does it? In this example, allow seven or eight minutes per essay, which will give you anywhere from 10 to 15 minutes to review, proofread, and make corrections and additions to all your answers. And if any of the questions are "weighted" more than the others, adjust the time you spend on them accordingly.

When the time you've budgeted for the first question is up, immediately move on to the next, no matter how far you've gotten on the first. You'll have time at the end—if you follow my suggestion—to go back and add more.

Most teachers will give you a better overall grade for five incomplete but decent essays than for three excellent ones and two left blank.

Don't ever, *ever* begin writing the answer to an essay question without a little "homework" first, even if you're the school's prize-winning journalist.

First, really look at the question. Are you sure you know what it's asking? Put it in your own words and compare it with your teacher's. Do they clearly mean the same thing? If not, you've misread it.

One way to avoid this problem is to paraphrase the question and make it the first sentence of your essay. Even if you have misread the teacher's question, you have shown her how *you* interpreted it. If you answer a slightly different question than the teacher intended, you may still get full credit for a well-written essay.

But please *don't*, intentionally or otherwise, misread the question in such a way that you answer the question you'd *like* rather than the one you've actually been given.

Make sure you understand the meaning of the "direction verbs." Don't "describe" when you've been told to "compare and contrast." Don't "explain" when you're supposed to "argue." See a list of the most-used such verbs and what each is instructing you to do later in this chapter.

A Foolproof Action Plan

Here's a step-by-step way to answer any essay question:

Step 1: On a blank sheet of paper, write down all the facts, ideas, concepts, and so forth, you feel should be included in your answer. (If you don't have extra paper, the back of your blue book or the test itself will work just as well.)

Step 2: Organize them in the order in which they should appear. You don't have to rewrite your notes into a detailed outline—just number each note according to where you want to place it in your essay.

Step 3: Compose your first paragraph. It should summarize and introduce the key points you will make in your essay. *This is where superior essay answers are made or unmade.*

Step 4: Write your essay, with your penmanship as legible as possible. Most teachers I've known do *not* attempt to decipher chicken scratch masquerading as an essay and do *not* award high grades to it either.

Step 5: Reread your essay and, if necessary, add points left out, correct spelling, grammar, and so on. Also watch for a careless omission that could cause serious damage—like leaving out a "not," for example, and making the point opposite the one you intended to write.

If there is a particular fact you know is important and should be included, but you just don't remember it, guess. Otherwise, just leave it out and do the best you can. If the rest of your essay is well thought out and organized and clearly communicates all the other points that should be included, I doubt most teachers will mark you down too severely for such an omission.

Don't set yourself up for a poor grade by making guesses you really don't have to. If you think something occurred in 1784, but are afraid it could be 1794, just write "in the late 18th century." You probably will *not* be marked down for the latter phrase, but *will* lose a point or two if you cite a wrong date.

Remember: Few teachers will be impressed by length. A well-organized, well-constructed, specific answer will always get you a better grade than writing down everything you know in the faint hope that you will actually include something pertinent. Writing a superior essay on the little you do know will usually earn you a better grade than knowing a lot and presenting it poorly.

Start out right, with a brief, to-the-point first paragraph that doesn't meander or "pad." End your essay with a clearly written and organized paragraph that offers more than just a summation of what you've already written.

Common Instructional Verbs on Essay Tests

Compare   Examine two or more objects, ideas, people, etc., and note similarities and differences.

Contrast   Compare to highlight differences.
                  Similar to *differentiate*, *distinguish*.

Criticize   Judge and discuss merits and faults.
                  Similar to *critique*.

Define   Explain the nature or essential qualities.

Describe   Convey appearance, nature, attributes, etc.

Discuss   Consider or examine by argument, comment, etc.; debate; explore solutions.

Enumerate   List various events, things, descriptions, ideas, etc.

Evaluate   Appraise the worth of an idea, comment, etc., and justify your conclusion.

Explain   Make the meaning of something clear, plain, intelligible, and/or understandable.

Illustrate   Use specific examples or analogies to explain.

Interpret   Give the meaning of something by paraphrase, by translation, or by an explanation based on personal opinion.

Justify   Defend a statement or conclusion.
                  Similar to *support*.

Narrate	Recount the occurrence of something, usually by giving details of events in the order in which they occurred. Similar to *describe*, but only applicable to something that happens in time.
Outline	Do a general sketch, account, or report, indicating only the main features of a book, subject, or project.
Prove	Establish the truth or genuineness by evidence or argument. Similar to *show*, *explain*, *demonstrate*. (In math, verify validity by mathematical demonstration.)
Relate	Give an account of events and/or circumstances, usually to establish association, connections, or relationships.
Review	Survey a topic, occurrence, or idea, generally but critically. Similar to *describe*, *discuss*, *illustrate*, *outline*, *summarize*, *trace*. Some test-makers may use these words virtually interchangeably, although one can find subtle differences in each.
State	Present the facts concisely and clearly. May be used interchangeably with *name*, *list*, *indicate*, *identify*, *enumerate*, *cite*.
Summarize	State in concise form, omitting examples and details.
Trace	Follow the course or history of an occurrence, idea, etc.

Worry less about the specific words and more about the information. Organize your answer to a fault and write to be understood, not to impress. Better to use shorter sentences, paragraphs, and words—and be clear and concise—than let the teacher fall into a clausal nightmare from which he may never emerge (and neither will your A!).

If you don't have the faintest clue what the question means, ask. If you still don't have any idea of the answer—and I mean *zilch*—leave it blank. Better to allocate more time to other parts of the test and do a better job on those.

Take time at the end of the test to review not only your essay answers, but your other answers as well. Make sure all words and numbers are readable. Make sure you have matched the right question to the right answer. Even make sure you didn't miss a whole section by turning over a page too quickly or not noticing that a page was missing. Make sure you can't, simply *can't*, add anything more to any of the essay answers.

What If Time Runs Out?

While you should have carefully allocated sufficient time to complete each essay before you started working on the first, things happen. You may find yourself with two minutes left and one full essay to go. What do you do? As quickly as possible, write down every piece of information you think should be included in your answer, and number each point in the order in which you would have written it. If you then have time to reorganize your notes into a clearer outline, do so. Many teachers will give you at least partial credit (some very near *full* credit) if your outline contains all the information the answer was supposed to. It will at least show you knew a lot about the subject and were capable of outlining a reasonable response.

One of the reasons you may have left yourself with insufficient time to answer one or more questions is you knew too darned much about the previous question(s). And you wanted to make sure the teacher *knew* you knew, so you wrote...and wrote...and wrote...until you ran out of time.

Be careful—some teachers throw in a relatively general question that, if you wanted to, you could write about until next Wednesday. In that case, they aren't testing your knowledge of the whole subject as much as your ability to *edit* yourself, to organize, and summarize the *important* points.

Standardized Tests

The various standardized tests used for college and graduate school admissions—the PSAT, SAT, ACT, LSAT, GRE—require their own pointers. These, like my oral exams at the end of four years of college, are not specific to any course or even one grade. Rather, they are attempting to assess your ability to apply mathematical concepts, read and understand various passages, and demonstrate language skills.

Despite their ephemeral nature, you *can* study for them by practicing. A solid review of English and math is essential. If you think geometry is just for squares, you'd better change your tune! Remember: As far as the PSAT and SAT are concerned, there is no penalty for guessing, so don't leave an answer blank!

Changes in the PSAT and SAT

Major changes in the SAT were introduced in 2005. It now consists of *three* sections: Writing (multiple-choice questions about grammar and usage *and an essay*); Critical Reading (formerly the "Verbal" section); and Math.

The new Writing section takes 1 hour—35 minutes for multiple-choice questions and 25 minutes to write an essay that requires you to take a position on an issue and use examples to support it. This section is marked (as the Verbal and Math sections still are) on a scale from 200 to 800, so a perfect SAT score is now 2,400. The SAT II: Writing Test was eliminated as of 2005.

The Critical Reading section now takes 70 minutes, broken down into two 25-minute sections and one 20-minute section. Analogies have been eliminated. Sentence-completion questions and long reading passages remain. Short reading passages were added.

The Math section also consists of two 25-minute sections and one 20-minute section. Quantitative comparison questions have been eliminated, but more advanced topics from algebra II—such as exponential growth, absolute value, and functional notation—were added. Calculators are still permitted (though it is still possible to solve every question without one).

As a result of these changes, the test now takes 3 hours and 45 minutes, 30 minutes longer than previous SAT exams.

Just to make sure everyone is confused, while some changes will be made to the PSAT, typically taken as practice by sophomores and juniors, it will include neither an essay nor advanced math. Go figure.

Put Me in, Coach

There are a variety of companies specializing in preparing students for each of these tests—your school might even sponsor its own course, and any bookstore will probably have shelves of preparation guides.

Should you take one of those SAT preparation courses? Is it worth the money, the time, the effort, the bother? According to a past study by the Educational Testing Service, which administers the SAT for the College Board, coached students who took the test twice or more increased their verbal score by 29 points, math by 40. Uncoached students showed an increase of 21 points on the verbal and 22 on math. These are the figures the College Board cites to claim that coaching does not really help.

Nevertheless, given their importance, I would recommend investing the time and money in any such reputable course—such as Stanley Kaplan, Princeton Review, BAR/BRI—or, at the very least, buying one of the major test-prep books.

Because these are, indeed, *standardized* tests, learning and utilizing specific techniques pertinent to them and practicing on tests given previously *can* significantly increase your scores, if only because you will feel less anxious and have a better idea of what's in store for you.

There are students who achieve exceptional test scores on their SATs and go on to compile barely adequate college records. These people are said to "test well": The testing environment doesn't throw them and they have sufficient prior experience to have an edge on the rest of the competition. Others "choke" during such tests but wind up at the top of the career pyramid.

You've probably been told for most of your life that your score on the SAT will determine whether you are a raving success eating in the finest restaurants or the busboy who cleans up afterwards. How vital is the SAT to the college admissions process and, one presumes, to the rest of your life? Depending on whom you listen to, "very" or "not at all."

According to Michele Hernandez, a former admissions officer at Dartmouth (quoted in the January 10, 1999, *New York Times Magazine*), "Deep down, admissions officers don't want SAT scores to count that much, but…they do." Yet more than 300 colleges no longer even require the SAT or ACT for admission, believing it's more important that they assess a student's real level of learning and effort, not their "innate ability."

Though one method of predicting success, such tests are not, by any means, perfect oracles. Nor are their conclusions inalienable. Many people have succeeded in life without ever doing particularly well on standardized tests.

Important Note: As of this writing, many standardized tests are no longer offered "on paper," only on computer (CAT—for computer-adaptive testing format). Among the most important that fall into this category are the GMAT (Graduate Management Admissions Test), GRE (Graduate Record Exam), and TOEFL (Test of English as a Foreign Language), along with a number of specific licensing tests.

What does this mean to you? Tests available only in CAT format require a different strategy because of two important factors: You can't return to a previous answer, and you can't skip a question and return to it later. Make sure you know if you are taking a computer or written test and practice (and strategize) accordingly!

A Special Note for Parents

Many parents take their children's grades and test scores far too seriously. Here's my advice to them:

1. Don't get overanxious about your child's test scores. Too much emphasis solely on grades can upset a child, especially one already chafing under too much pressure.

2. Children who are afraid of failing are more likely to make mistakes on tests. Help them feel confident about everything they do.

3. Don't judge your child by a single test score, no matter how important the test. No test is a perfect measure of what a child can do or what she has actually learned.

4. Talk to your child's teacher as often as possible. Her assessment will be a far better measure of how your child is doing than any test, or even any series of tests.

5. Make sure your child attends school regularly. You can't do well on tests if you are rarely in class.

6. Make sure your child gets enough sleep, especially before a big test. Tired eyes lead to tired grades.

7. Review test results with your child and show him what he can learn from a graded exam paper. This is especially crucial in math and the sciences, where a new concept builds upon the previous ones.

8. Look at the wrong answers. Find out why she answered as she did. This will identify times when your child knew the right answer but didn't fully understand the question.

9. Read and discuss any teacher comments on the test, especially if your child received a poor grade.

Pretest Organizer

Class: _____ **Teacher:** _____

Test date: _____ **Time:** From: _____ To: _____

Place: _____

Special instructions to myself (e.g., take calculator, dictionary, etc.):

_____

_____

_____

_____

_____

_____

Materials I need to study for this test (check all needed):

_____ Book   _____ DVDs/videos

_____ Workbook   _____ Old tests

_____ Class notes   _____ Other

_____ Handouts

Format of the test (write the number of T/F, essays, and so forth, and total points for each section):

_____

_____

_____

_____

_____

_____

_____

Study group meetings (times, places):

1. _____
2. _____
3. _____
4. _____
5. _____
6. _____
7. _____
8. _____

Material to be covered:

Indicate topics, sources, and amount of review (light or heavy) required. Check when review is completed.

Topic	Sources	Review
_____	_____	_____
_____	_____	_____
_____	_____	_____
_____	_____	_____
_____	_____	_____
_____	_____	_____
_____	_____	_____
_____	_____	_____

After the test:

Grade I expected _____   Grade I received _____

What did I do that helped me?

_____

_____

_____

_____

_____

_____

_____

_____

_____

What else should I have done?

_____

_____

_____

_____

_____

_____

_____

_____

_____

EPILOGUE

I'm proud of you. You made it all the way through the book. Here's my final advice:

- Reread *How to Study,* cover to cover. It's similar to seeing a movie for the second time—you always find something you missed the first time around.
- Practice what I preached. You had an *excuse* for flunking before—you didn't know how to study. Now you have absolutely *no* excuse.
- Buy, read, and put into practice whichever of the companion volumes you need.
- Write me a letter to tell me what helped, how much better you're doing in school, or to let me know what else I can include to add to the value of the books.

Send your letters to:

> Ron Fry
> c/o Career Press
> P.O. Box 687
> Franklin Lakes, NJ 07417

I promise I'll try to respond if you ask, but please avoid calling me—I'll probably be on the road promoting *How to Study*! Good studying!

INDEX

15 minutes daily, setting aside for planning, 93
80-20 Rule, 25

A

action verbs, using in papers, 163
active listening, 112
active voice, using in papers, 163
Amazon, searching, 130
American Firsts example, 6–7
Anxiety Quotient (AQ), lowering, 174–175
appendices, explained, 48
AQ (Anxiety Quotient), lowering, 174–175
argument, presenting in oral reports, 168
assignments
    completing for classes, 107–108
    considering complexity of, 37
"aural" students, preferences of, 28

B

bibliographies
    explained, 47
    preparing for papers, 165–166
bibliography cards, using for papers, 144–147
book catalogs, using for research, 126

book elements
    appendices, 48
    bibliography, 47
    footnotes, 47
    glossary, 47
    introduction, 47
    preface, 47
books. *See* fiction elements; textbooks
boredom, fighting, 40
brainstorming, using with research papers, 158
breaks, taking, 29, 32, 39
de la Bruyere, Jean, 75

C

calendars
    color coding, 90
    daily, 83–85, 96–99
    including research papers on, 138–139
    long-term, 83, 94
card catalog, using for research, 125
CAT (computer-adaptive testing), 211
chapters
    completing, 54
    elements of, 49–50
    formats of, 49–50
    reading headings in, 49

chapters *(continued)*
  reading summaries of, 49
  using clues in, 49–50
  See also reading; textbooks
characterization, explained, 60
class participation
  assessing, 11
  scoring, 11
classes
  active participation in, 118–120
  asking questions in, 104, 112
  attending regularly, 121
  avoiding distracting classmates, 110
  completing assignments for,
    107–108
  discussions, 102–103
  excelling in, 119
  follow-up tasks, 120–121
  "Grade A" approach, 118–120
  having questions ready for, 108
  lectures, 102
  listening for verbal clues, 110–111
  minimizing distractions in, 109
  picking, 42
  preparing attitude for, 109
  preparing for, 107–109
  reviewing notes for, 108
  seminars, 102–103
  sitting near front in, 109–110
  taking notes in, 112–113
  tutorials, 102–103
  uncategorized, 103–104
  watching for nonverbal clues, 111
classmates, listening to, 120
classroom, concentrating in, 29
commuters, time management for,
    92
compare, using in essays, 205
comprehension questions, answer-
    ing on tests, 196
comprehension skills, testing, 6–7
computer databases, using for
    research, 126
computer skills
  assessing, 10
  scoring, 10

computer-adaptive testing (CAT),
    211
concentration, maintaining, 91
conclusion, writing for papers, 162
confidence, building, 120
contrast, using in essays, 205
Cornell note-taking system, using,
    117
courses, picking, 42
cramming for tests, 180–182
The Creative Guide to Research,
    130–132
crib sheets, making for tests, 179
criticize, using in essays, 205

D

days, planning ahead of time, 89
de la Bruyere, Jean, 75
define, using in essays, 205
denouement, defined, 60
Descartes, Rene, 72
describe, using in essays, 205
Dewey decimal system
  history classification, 127
  mathematics classification, 128
  philosophy classification, 127
  use by libraries, 127–128
discuss, using in essays, 205
discussions, primary emphases,
    102–103
distractions
  managing while studying, 91–92
  minimizing in classes, 111

E

Eliot, T. S., 1
encyclopedias, using for research,
    123
enumerate, using in essays, 205
essay questions, appearance on
    tests, 184
essay tests
  action plan, 203–204
  guessing on, 204
  instructional verbs on, 205

paraphrasing questions on, 203
reviewing, 207
running out of time on, 207–208
starting, 204
taking, 202–207
explain, using in essays, 205
Exploring Feng Shui example,
    61–63
extrinsic motivation, 21–22

F

**facts, checking in research papers,
    163**
fiction elements
    characterization, 60
    plot, 60
    point of view, 60
    reading, 60
    setting, 60
    theme, 60
    understanding, 61
footnotes
    explained, 47
    including in papers, 159–160
foreign language texts, reading, 59
forgetting, reasons for, 70–71
**freewriting, using with research
    papers, 158**
Fry paper-writing system, 137–138

G

Gibaldi, Joseph, 146
Gide, Andre, 60
glossary, explained, 47
**GMAT (Graduate Management
    Admissions Test), 211**
goal pyramid, constructing, 22–24
goal-setting, 87–88
**government publications, using for
    research, 126**
**"Grade A" approach, following,
    118–120**
graphics, examining, 51
GRE (Graduate Record Exam), 211

H

habits
    reinforcing good, 89
    replacing bad with good, 16–17
Hacker, Diana, 146
**hands-on classes, primary
    emphases, 103**
**headings, rephrasing as questions,
    51**
Hernandez, Michele, 211
homework assignments
    doing and turning in, 108
    including on calendar, 84
How? question, answering, 54

I

illustrate, using in essays, 205
illustrations, examining, 51
index cards
    adding detail to, 149–150
    creating for research papers, 149
    organizing, 151–154
    reviewing, 154
    using for bibliographies, 144–147
    using for oral reports, 168–169
    using to write first drafts, 155–156
information, receiving, 29
**instructional verbs, using in
    essays, 205–206**
instructions, reading, 19
instructors
    adapting to styles of, 106–107
    compiling "profiles" of, 20
    considering reputations of, 43
    following instructions of, 19
    knowing, 104–106
    response to presentation, 20
    understanding goals of, 105–106
Internet, using for research, 126.
    See also **online research**
interpret, using in essays, 205
interruptions, managing, 91–92
intrinsic motivation, 21–22

introduction
  explained, 47
  writing for papers, 162

J

justify, using in essays, 205

K

key words, identifying in technical
  texts, 56. *See also* word clues
kids, studying with, 40–41

L

Law of Diminishing Returns, 27
lectures, primary emphases,
  102–103
libraries
  Dewey decimal system, 127
  organization of, 127–129
  studying at, 34
library, building one's own, 72–73
Library of Congress system,
  128–129
library research, beginning,
  142–143
library skills
  evaluating, 9
  scoring, 9
"listening" versus "seeing," 28

M

math tests, multiple-choice,
  198–200
memorizing versus understanding,
  70
Mitchell, Shawne, 61–63
MLA (Modern Language Association), 146
MLA guidelines, following, 160
motivation, intrinsic and extrinsic,
  21–22

motivators, using rewards as, 24
multiple-choice tests
  acing, 191–192
  strategy, 193–195
multitasking, 82

N

naps, taking, 40
narrate, using in essays, 206
newspaper indexes, using for
  research, 126
note cards
  adding detail to, 149–150
  creating for research papers, 149
  organizing, 151–154
  reviewing, 154
  using for bibliographies, 144–145,
    147
  using for oral reports, 168–169
  using to write first drafts, 155–156
note taking, 71
  adapting to teachers' styles, 106
  in class, 10–11
  in classes, 112–113
  Cornell system, 117
  guidelines, 114
  in library, 11
  M (My thought) symbol, 116
  mapping, 117–118
  online, 11
  scoring skills, 11
  skills assessment, 10–11
  streamlining, 114–117
  T! (Test!) symbol, 116
  from textbooks, 10
  on unknown information, 113–114
  using diagrams, 117–118
  using drawings, 117–118
  using shorthand for, 114–117
  using symbols in, 116
  W (What?) symbol, 116
  while reading, 68–69
notes, reviewing for classes, 108

O

online information, citing in papers, 146
online research, approach to, 129–132. *See also* **Internet**
oral reports
  argument, 168
  avoiding overuse of statistics, 169
  description, 168
  exposition, 168
  narration, 168
  practicing, 170
  preparing, 12
  using quotes, 169
organization
  80-20 Rule, 25
  making small changes, 24–25
  maximizing "in-between" time, 26
  Pareto Principle, 25
organizational plan. *See* **time management**
outline, using in essays, 206
outlines
  adding details to, 151–154
  developing for research papers, 143

P

papers
  adding personal notes, 150–151
  beginning library research, 142–143
  brainstorming, 158
  checking facts, 163
  checking spelling, 166
  choosing topics for, 140–141
  choosing search engines for, 130
  citing online information in, 146
  considering topics for, 140–141
  consulting *Who's Who* series, 124
  creating bibliography, 144–145
  creating temporary outlines, 143
  creating work schedules for, 138–139
  dealing with writer's block, 157
  developing temporary thesis, 142–143

  documenting sources, 158–159
  doing additional research, 160
  editing for meaning, 160–165
  evaluating resources, 124–125
  final draft, 167
  following instructions for, 134–135
  freewriting, 158
  Fry paper-writing system, 137–138
  fundamental rules for, 134
  getting proofread, 167
  including footnotes in, 159–160
  including topic sentences, 156
  note-taking guidelines, 149
  online resources, 129–130
  organizing note cards, 151–154
  organizing paragraphs in, 155–156
  preparing bibliographies for, 165–166
  preparing detailed outlines, 151–154
  preparing to take notes, 148
  presentation of, 136
  primary versus secondary resources, 124–125
  proofreading, 166
  reviewing first drafts, 160
  reviewing note cards, 154
  reworking paragraphs, 162
  rewriting, 163–165
  setting aside time for, 126
  starting, 123
  substance and form of, 19–20
  turning in on time, 135
  using action verbs, 163
  using active voice, 163
  using descriptive words, 164
  using encyclopedias, 123
  using for future reference, 136–137
  varying sentence structure, 165
  writing, 12
  writing conclusions, 162
  writing first drafts of, 154–160
  writing introductions, 162
  writing second drafts, 160–165
  See also research-paper sources

paragraphs
closing, 162
opening, 162
organizing in papers, 155–156
reworking in second drafts, 162
parents, advice about testing, 212
Pareto Principle, 25
Parkinson's Law, 89
perfectionists, traits of, 26–27
periodical indexes, using for research, 126
plagiarism, avoiding in papers, 158–159
planning
according to schedule, 89
next day, 89
pleasurable activities, 90
plot, explained, 60
point of view, explained, 60
preface, explained, 47
prereading, importance of, 50–52. *See also* **reading**
pressure, performing under, 31
Pretest Organizer, 213–215
primary resources, using in research, 125
Priority Task Sheet
example, 95, 98
using, 86–87
professors. *See* **teachers**
projects, including on calendar, 84
prove, using in essays, 206
The Publication Manual of the APA, 146

Q

questionnaire
evaluating answers to, 4
responding to, 2–3
questions
asking in classes, 112
preparing for classes, 108

R

***Reader's Guide to Periodical Literature*, 142**
reading
actively, 69
aesthetic, 50, 60–61
asking questions before, 69
components, 6
comprehension, 6
critical, 50
defining purpose for, 46, 51
details, 53–54
developing good habits, 70
fiction, 60
five questions, 53–54
foreign language texts, 59
How? question, 54
introductory paragraphs, 52
memory systems, 68
organizing material, 70
with a plan, 57–59
pleasure, 50, 60–61
purpose for, 46
recall, 6, 67–68
recognition, 68
reference, 50
remembering, 65–66, 71–72
repetition for recall, 68
retention, 7–8, 66–67
scoring pace of, 61
seeking word clues, 52–53
skimming versus scanning, 51
speed, 6
speed versus comprehension, 67
taking notes, 68–69
technical texts, 54–59
"top-of-the-mind" recall, 6–7
using clues in textbooks, 46–48
ways of, 50
When? question, 53
Where? question, 53
Who? question, 53
Why? question, 54
writing definitions of terms, 54
See also chapters; prereading

reading assignments
    completing for classes, 107–108
    starting, 49–50
reading factors
    association, 66
    desire, 66
    overlearning, 66
    systematizing, 66
    understanding, 65
reading skills
    scoring, 7
    testing, 6–7
reading speed
    decreasing, 63
    increasing, 63–64
    measuring, 61
    scoring, 61
    testing, 61–63
recall, process of, 67–68
relate, using in essays, 206
reports. *See* **research papers**
Research and Documentation in the
    Electronic Age, **146**
research papers
    adding personal notes, 150–151
    beginning library research, 142–143
    brainstorming, 158
    checking facts, 163
    checking spelling, 166
    choosing topics for, 140–141
    choosing search engines for, 130
    citing online information in, 146
    considering topics for, 140–141
    consulting *Who's Who* series, 124
    creating bibliography, 144–145
    creating temporary outlines, 143
    creating work schedules for,
        138–139
    dealing with writer's block, 157
    developing temporary thesis,
        142–143
    documenting sources, 158–159
    doing additional research, 160

    editing for meaning, 160–165
    evaluating resources, 124–125
    final draft, 167
    following instructions for, 134–135
    freewriting, 158
    Fry paper-writing system, 137–138
    fundamental rules for, 134
    getting proofread, 167
    including footnotes in, 159–160
    including topic sentences, 156
    note-taking guidelines, 149
    online resources, 129–130
    organizing note cards, 151–154
    organizing paragraphs in, 155–156
    preparing bibliographies for,
        165–166
    preparing detailed outlines, 151–154
    preparing to take notes, 148
    presentation of, 136
    primary versus secondary
        resources, 124–125
    proofreading, 166
    reviewing first drafts, 160
    reviewing note cards, 154
    reworking paragraphs, 162
    rewriting, 163–165
    setting aside time for, 126
    starting, 123
    substance and form of, 19–20
    turning in on time, 135
    using action verbs, 163
    using active voice, 163
    using descriptive words, 164
    using encyclopedias, 123
    using for future reference, 136–137
    varying sentence structure, 165
    writing, 12
    writing conclusions, 162
    writing first drafts of, 154–160
    writing introductions, 162
    writing second drafts, 160–165

research-paper sources
book catalogs, 126
card catalog, 125
computer databases, 126
government publications, 126
Internet, 126
newspaper indexes, 126
periodical indexes, 126
vertical files, 126
retention, process of, 66–67
retention skills
scoring, 8
testing, 7–8
review, using in essays, 206
rewards, using as motivators, 24
Rowland, Robin, 130–132

S
SAT
changes in, 208–209
Critical Reading section, 208–209
Math section, 208–209
preparation courses, 210
Writing section, 208–209
scanning versus skimming, 51–52
scores, evaluating for initial assessment, 13
search engines, choosing for research, 130
secondary resources, using in research, research–project sources, 125
"seeing" versus "listening," 28
self-testing, 185–186
seminars, primary emphases, 102–103
setting, explained, 60
shy students, tip for, 120
Simenon, George, 27
skimming
versus scanning, 51–52
tests, 186

sleep habits, considering, 36
sources, documenting for research papers, 158–159
spelling, checking in research papers, 166
Spignesi, Stephen, 6–7
standardized tests, taking, 208–211
state, using in essays, 206
studies, staying focused on, 39
study breaks, taking, 29, 32, 39
study clock, knowing, 91
study environment
creating, 28–32, 39
evaluating, 38
study groups
organizing, 32–34
participating in, 32–34
study habits
assessing, 4–5
developing, 16–17
study pace, setting, 43
study schedule
changing, 40
setting, 37
study sequence, identifying, 18
"To Study" sheets, creating for tests, 185
study skills
evaluating, 2–5
questionnaire, 2–3
questionnaire results, 4
study strategy, identifying, 18
study strengths, determining, 42
study symbol, selecting, 39
study time, scheduling, 88–89
studying
charting time for, 80–81
choosing times for, 36–37
considering sleep habits, 36
in empty classrooms, 35
with friends, 35

at home, 35
at jobs, 35
at library, 34
as lifelong process, 17–19
with small kids, 40–41
smarter, 15–16
subheadings, examining, 51
subject areas, evaluation of, 44
success, concentrating on, 43
summarize, using in essays, 206
symbol, selecting for studying, 39

T

table of contents, 47
taking notes, 71
adapting to teachers' styles, 106
in class, 10–11
in classes, 112–113
Cornell system, 117
guidelines, 114
in library, 11
M (My thought) symbol, 116
mapping, 117–118
online, 11
scoring skills, 11
skills assessment, 10–11
streamlining, 114–117
T! (Test!) symbol, 116
from textbooks, 10
on unknown information, 113–114
using diagrams, 117–118
using drawings, 117–118
using shorthand for, 114–117
using symbols in, 116
W (What?) symbol, 116
while reading, 68–69
tasks
prioritizing, 86–90
scheduling time for, 88

teachers
adapting to styles of, 106–107
compiling "profiles" of, 20
considering reputations of, 43
following instructions of, 19
knowing, 104–106
response to presentation, 20
understanding goals of, 105–106
technical texts
cause-effect relationships, 55–57
classifications, 55–56
comparing and contrasting, 55–56
creating drawings, 59
definitions and terms, 55
estimating answers, 59
examples, 55–56
focusing on retention, 58
key words, 56
learning terms, 57
listings, 55–56
organizational devices, 54–57
reading, 54–59
reading analytically, 58
reading thoroughly, 58
reading with a plan, 57–59
reviewing after reading, 58
rewording content, 58
skimming chapters, 58
teaching others, 59
tricks, 58–59
working backwards, 59
See also textbooks
term papers
adding personal notes, 150–151
beginning library research, 142–143
brainstorming, 158
checking facts, 163
checking spelling, 166
choosing topics for, 140–141
choosing search engines for, 130

term papers *(continued)*
citing online information in, 146
considering topics for, 140–141
consulting *Who's Who* series, 124
creating bibliography, 144–145
creating temporary outlines, 143
creating work schedules for, 138–139
dealing with writer's block, 157
developing temporary thesis, 142–143
documenting sources, 158–159
doing additional research, 160
editing for meaning, 160–165
evaluating resources, 124–125
final draft, 167
following instructions for, 134–135
freewriting, 158
Fry paper-writing system, 137–138
fundamental rules for, 134
getting proofread, 167
including footnotes in, 159–160
including topic sentences, 156
note-taking guidelines, 149
online resources, 129–130
organizing note cards, 151–154
organizing paragraphs in, 155–156
preparing bibliographies for, 165–166
preparing detailed outlines, 151–154
preparing to take notes, 148
presentation of, 136
primary versus secondary resources, 124–125
proofreading, 166
reviewing first drafts, 160
reviewing note cards, 154
reworking paragraphs, 162
rewriting, 163–165
setting aside time for, 126
starting, 123
substance and form of, 19–20
turning in on time, 135
using action verbs, 163

using active voice, 163
using descriptive words, 164
using encyclopedias, 123
using for future reference, 136–137
varying sentence structure, 165
writing, 12
writing conclusions, 162
writing first drafts of, 154–160
writing introductions, 162
writing second drafts, 160–165
See also research-paper sources
test anxiety
common experience of, 173
dealing with, 172
minimizing, 175
protecting oneself from, 174
relaxation techniques, 175–176
test day, rules and reminders, 186–191
Test of English as a Foreign Language (TOEFL), 211
test preparation, 12–13
testing oneself, 185–186
tests
advice to parents, 212
"All of the above" option, 195
allocating study time for, 180
asking teachers about, 182–184
avoiding cramming for, 180–182
changing guesses, 189–190
creating "To Study" sheets for, 185
discriminate and eliminate, 188–189
drawing pictures during, 187
essay questions, 184
following instructions for, 190
guessing on, 188–189
knowing rules for, 187
making crib sheet, 179
materials, 178
multiple-choice, 191–195
multiple-choice math, 198–200
"None of the above" option, 195
objective questions on, 184

open-book, 200–201
optional assignments, 178
organizing material, 179
planning for, 176
practicing, 185
Pretest Organizer, 213–215
reading comprehension questions,
    195–196
rechecking answers, 191
reviewing for, 176–179
skimming, 186
standardized, 208–211
take-home, 201–202
true/false, 197–198
using two alarm clocks, 177
weighted sections, 187
writing essays, 202–207
textbook elements
appendices, 48
bibliography, 47
footnotes, 47
glossary, 47
introduction, 47
preface, 47
table of contents, 47
textbooks
finding alternatives, 48–49
using clues in, 46–48
See also technical texts
theme, explained, 60
**thesaurus, consulting for papers,
    164**
**thesis statement, developing for
    papers, 142–143**
time management
15-minute daily planning, 93
benefits of, 76–78
charting available time, 80–82
collecting materials for, 82
for commuters, 92
daily calendar, 83–85

handling distractions, 91
identifying starting line, 80–82
limitation, 78–79
long-term planning calendar, 83
monitoring progress, 90
planning, 79, 89
prioritizing tasks, 86–88
Priority Task Sheet, 86–87, 95, 98
of research projects, 126
weekly planning, 85–86
Where Does Your Time Go? chart,
    81
time management skills
assessing, 8
maximizing, 26
tiredness, fighting, 40
**TOEFL (Test of English as a
    Foreign Language), 211**
**topic sentences, including in
    papers, 156**
**"top-of-the-mind" recall, assessing,
    6–7**
trace, using in essays, 206
true/false tests, taking, 197–198
**tutorials, primary emphases,
    102–103**

U

**understanding versus memorizing,
    70**

V

verbs, using in essays, 205–206
**vertical files, using for research,
    126**
**"visual" students, preferences of,
    28**

W

When? question, answering, 53
Where Does Your Time Go? chart,
    81
Where? question, answering, 53
Who? question, answering, 53
Who's Who series, consulting for
    research, 124
Why? question, answering, 54
word clues, seeking, 52–53. *See
    also* key words
writer's block, overcoming, 157
writing, essence of, 155
writing papers, 12
writing skills, scoring, 11

About the Author

Ron Fry is a nationally known spokesperson for the improvement of public education and an advocate for parents and students playing an active role in strengthening personal education programs. Aside from being the author of the vastly popular *How to Study Program*, Fry has edited or written more than 30 different titles — resources for optimum student success.

"Helpful for students of all ages from high school and up."
– Small Press Book Review

"These are must-read guides every family should have in its library."
– Library Journal

How to Study Series:

- **How to Study**
- **"Ace" Any Test**
- **Get Organized**
- **Improve Your Memory**
- **Improve Your Writing**
- **Improve Your Reading**

*For product information and technology assistance,
contact us at*

*Cengage Learning Customer & Sales Support,
1-800-354-9706.*